808.8
H 339c
f

THE HARVARD CLASSICS

The Five-Foot Shelf of Books

*Statue of John Harvard before University Hall,
Harvard University, Cambridge, Massachusetts*

THE HARVARD CLASSICS
EDITED BY CHARLES W. ELIOT, LL.D.

Fifteen Minutes a Day

The Reading Guide

P. F. Collier & Son Company
NEW YORK

The Purpose of
This Book

THIS book was prepared and is sent to you with one purpose in view, to enable you to profit in full measure from the writings of the immortals whom you have at your beck and call in the Harvard Classics.

This great company of the wisest, the wittiest, the most interesting minds of all ages and every land will afford you entertainment in endless variety, inspiration and stimulation of mind. They will carry you forward upon that road to the high goal toward which all of us are making our way. It is then to the countless hours in which you will walk in step with these great thinkers of all time that this book is dedicated.

The Harvard Classics are "all things to all men." They are universal in their appeal and universal in their power to bestow pleasure, self satisfaction and the joy of mental growth to each man, woman and child with impartiality and in infinite variety.

What Shall I Read Tonight?

HOW often does that question come to all of us? Magazines, newspapers, the books of the day—all pall upon us with their deadly monotony of the commonplace. We want something to carry us out of ourselves, to take us a million miles from our humdrum existence, to stimulate our minds to fresh endeavor, to give us a new viewpoint upon our problems, to enable us to get a fresh hold upon ourselves.

Then it is, that the Harvard Classics find their place. They meet every need, they entertain when no other book can, they exhilarate and they satisfy. They bring to you the rare pleasure of commingling with great minds, they feed your mind with stimulating thoughts, they turn your mind into fresh channels. For the Harvard Classics touch every facet of human interest. Here beckoning to you are romance, adventure, drama and mystery. Read to your heart's content in these full blooded books—full of thrill, stimulus and delight.

The Never-Ceasing Fascination of These Books

You can turn to the Arabian Nights, to the explorations of Drake and Raleigh, to the adventures of Ulysses, to the homely philosophy of Franklin, to Froissart's entrancing Chronicles, to the breathless poems of Browning, to the writings of the prophets of the mystic east, to the glorious moving prose of Burke and Macaulay, and so on through the great classics of the ages.

We want to urge you to keep at all times several volumes of the Harvard Classics easily at hand on your desk or table to read and to browse through. Don't put your set away in a distant bookcase where you must go to get them. These are friendly books to have near you, they are the best of companions at all times. To be able to reach for your favorite volume and take a few moments out of a busy day, in which you are transported to other worlds and other times is a privilege that cannot be held lightly. The Harvard Classics will repay you manyfold in dividends of delight and satisfaction for the hours you have spent in the company of the immortal writers.

How Dr. Eliot Solved Your Reading Problem

DR. CHARLES W. ELIOT for forty years President of Harvard University, acclaimed without question America's greatest scholar and educator, was eminently fitted to select out of the world's literature, a well-rounded library of liberal education—depicting the progress of man observing, recording, inventing, and imagining from the earliest historical times to the present day.

Never before had a task of this magnitude been undertaken by an educator of the standing of Dr. Eliot. Never before had a question of such unusual public importance received the time and attention that has been applied to the selection of the contents of the Harvard Classics.

Dr. Eliot's Own Story of the Five-Foot Shelf

"Before the reading plan represented by The Harvard Classics had taken definite form, I had more than once stated in public that in my opinion a five-foot—at first a three-foot—shelf would hold books enough to afford a good substitute for a liberal education to anyone who would read them with devotion, even if he could spare but fifteen minutes a day for reading.

"P. F. Collier & Son Company proposed that I undertake to make a selection of fifty volumes, which would approximately fill a five-foot shelf, and be well adapted to accomplish the educational object I had in mind.

"I accepted the proposal. The work of selection extended inter-mittently over nearly twelve months; for the question of exclusion or inclusion of each item had to be carefully considered from every possible angle.

Harvard University Sanctions the Title

"It was further proposed that the set be called the Harvard Classics. In view of this proposed name, and of the fact that I had been president of Harvard University for nearly forty years, I asked the President and Fellows of Harvard College if they saw any objec-tion, from the point of view of the University, to my accepting the proposal of P. F. Collier & Son Company. The Board replied unanimously that they saw no objection, and that, in their judgment, the undertaking, if well carried out, would prove a useful one from the educational point of view.

Dr. Eliot's Aim

"My aim was not to select the best fifty, or best hundred, books in the world, but to give, in twenty-three thousand pages or thereabouts, a picture of the progress of the human race within historical times, so far as that progress can be depicted in books. The purpose of The Harvard Classics is, therefore, one different from that of collections in which the editor's aim has been to select a number of best books; it is nothing less than the purpose to present so ample and characteristic a record of the stream of the world's thought that the observant reader's mind shall be enriched, refined and fertilized.

"Within the limits of fifty volumes, containing about twenty-three thousand pages, my task was to provide the means of obtaining such knowledge of ancient and modern literature as seemed essential to the twentieth-century idea of a cultivated man. The best acquisition of a cultivated man is a liberal frame of mind or way of thinking; but there must be added to that possession acquaintance with the prodigious store of recorded discoveries, experiences, and reflections which humanity in its intermittent and irregular progress from barbarism to civilization has acquired and laid up.

Liberal Education Defined

"Liberal education accomplishes two objects. It produces a liberal frame of mind, and it makes the studious and reflective recipient acquainted with the stream of the world's thought and feeling, and with the infinitely varied products of the human imagination. It was my hope and belief that fifty volumes might accomplish this result for any intelligent, ambitious, and persistent reader, whether his early opportunities for education has been large or small. Such was the educational purpose with which I undertook to edit The Harvard Classics.

"All the main divisions of literature are represented. Chronologically considered, the series begins with portions of the sacred books of the oldest religions, proceeds with specimens of the literature of Greece and Rome, then makes selections from the literature of the Middle Ages in the Orient, Italy, France, Scandinavia, Ireland, England, Germany and the Latin Church, includes a considerable representation of the literature of the Renaissance in Italy, France, Germany, England, Scotland and Spain, and arriving at modern times comprehends selections derived from Italy, three centuries of France, two centuries of Germany, three centuries of England and something more than a century of the United States.

"In order to make the best use of The Harvard Classics it will be desirable for the reader to reread those volumes or passages which he finds most interesting, and commit to memory many of the pieces of poetry which stir and uplift him. It is a source of exquisite and enduring delight to have one's mind stored with many melodious expressions of high thoughts and beautiful imagery.

"The elaborate alphabetical index is intended to give any person immediate access to any author or any subject mentioned in the entire collection, and indeed to any passage in the fifty volumes to which the inquirer has a good clue. This full index makes The Harvard Classics convenient books of reference.

Coöperation of Harvard University

"It would have been impossible to perform the task satisfactorily if the treasures of the general library and of the department libraries of Harvard University had not been at disposal. The range of the topics in the series was so wide, and the number of languages in which the desired books were originally written so great, that the advice of specialists, each in some portion of the field, had frequently to be sought. I obtained much valuable advice of this sort from scholarly friends and neighbors.

* * * *

"The Harvard Classics have demonstrated their fitness for the special work they were intended to do. The publishers have advised me that nearly a half million sets have been placed in the homes of enthusiastic purchasers, and that a stream of unsolicited letters of approval comes from these owners. I have myself been surprised to see how often I turn to the collection to enjoy pieces of permanent literature, in contrast with the mass of ephemeral reading matter which I am obliged to go through.

"One may hope that the collection will endure for decades to come, not only as a monument and milestone, but also as an active force toward the sound mental equipment of American reading people."

Charles W. Eliot

The Harvard Classics Embrace the Sum-Total of Literature and Life

DR. ELIOT'S Five-Foot Shelf of Books free you from the limitations of your age, of your country, of your personal experiences; they give you access to all ages, to all countries, to all experience. They take you out of the rut of life in the town you live in and make you a citizen of the world. They offer you the companionship of the most interesting and influential men and women who have ever lived; they make it possible for you to travel without leaving home, and to have vacations without taking time from your work. They offer you—if you will only accept their gifts—friends, travel, the knowledge of life; they offer you education, the means of making your life what you want it to be.

Emerson said: "There are 850,000 volumes in the Imperial Library at Paris. If a man were to read industriously from dawn to dark for sixty years, he would die in the first alcove. Would that some charitable soul, after losing a great deal of time among the false books and alighting upon a few true ones, which made him happy and wise, would name those which have been bridges or ships to carry him safely over dark morasses and barren oceans, into the heart of sacred cities, into palaces and temples."

Emerson's wish, which is the great need and wish of thousands of earnest, ambitious people, has been fulfilled. The fulfillment is Dr. Eliot's Five-Foot Shelf of Books.

What The Five-Foot Shelf Brings To You

NOW you have the Harvard Classics, stop for a moment and think just what they mean to you! Dr. Eliot's Five-Foot Shelf of Books bring to your side, in the comfort of your own home, a liberal education, entertainment and counsel of the greatest men the world has ever seen.

These men are the makers of civilization, the shapers of history. You live with them through past ages; you know their achievements; you travel with them, discover with them, hear their immortal sayings, listen to their profound logic, thrill to their beautiful poems and stories.

The world's immortals stand ready to take you into their confidence. You can live with them day by day. You can watch Cellini—wonderful combination of artist and knave—in his dealings with princes and pontiffs, his love affairs and his duels. You can read the letters of Pliny the Younger, in which he asks whether he shall destroy the "sect called Christians," and those describing the destruction of Pompeii. You can stand with Cicero in the Roman Senate while he denounces Catiline. You revel in the delightful humor of the eccentric Don Quixote, who gaily set forth to battle windmills, believing that they were giants.

Here Are Romance, Humor and Adventure

You will thrill again to the adventures of the Boy Dana, standing on the windswept deck of his sailing ship as she encountered the hazardous passage around Cape Horn. You will respond to the lilt of Herrick's poem, as he writes, "Gather ye rosebuds while ye may, Old Time is still a-flying." You will read the fascinating oriental adventures to be found in The Thousand and One Nights. You can see Franklin hanging out the lantern in front of his house, the first street light in America. You can live with the greatest men in the intimate personal concerns of their daily existence. There is in all literature no greater pleasure than this.

By opening the pages of a book, to transport oneself in a second into the age of Pericles or the Gardens of the Medici at Florence, is the modern version of Aladdin's lamp and makes one master of treasures more rare and lustrous than those which adorned the palaces of Bagdad.

Dr. Eliot's selections cover every field of human knowledge. On the authority of this great educator and scholar, you have at your elbow the most interesting and important books.

So vast is the range of The Harvard Classics, that they touch every phase of human interest. They tell of the great discoveries and inventions of the ages, the epoch-making progress of our world in science and medicine, and they relate the history and development of our laws, our educational systems, and our humanitarian reforms. They present the supreme works of 302 of the world's immortal, creative minds; essays, biography, fiction, history, philosophy, the supreme writings which express man's ambitions, hope and development throughout the centuries.

"My first reading of the Harvard Classics," writes a woman purchaser, "gave me a pleasure likened unto finding small particles of gold, and the more I read, the more nuggets of golden literature are obtained through a few minutes of pleasant reading each day." Nearly a half million busy men and women are finding the joy of mental relaxation and stimulus in a few moments a day spent with these books.

The Magnificent Special Features in
The Harvard Classics

WHAT makes the Harvard Classics the greatest library of literature ever conceived? What has brought these marvelous works into the homes of nearly a half million people? The Harvard Classics most assuredly have supreme qualities that entitle them to greatness. Dr. Eliot has given in this peerless library two incomparable boons to the world.

The first has been to present a brilliant selection of the priceless writings of all time so that, as he said, "Their faithful and considerate reading will give any man the essentials of a liberal education, even if he devote but fifteen minutes a day." The second is found in the magnificent group of editorial features. These are:

> The Introductory Lectures
> The Footnotes
> The General Index
> The Index to the First Lines
> The Chronological Index
> The Readers' Guide
> The Selections for Boys and Girls
> The Lecture Volume
> The Daily Reading Guide

These make the Harvard Classics live to the reader, they indispensably aid him to obtain the utmost in enjoyment from his set. They transform these imperishable books into a living, constructive force to entertain, stimulate and inspire him. They enable the Harvard Classics to render an educational service unsurpassed by any other set of books.

In brief, these great exclusive features combined with the priceless selections give to every man and woman the privilege of a university training at home. These invaluable features are described in detail in the following pages.

Introductory Lectures

IN leafing through the volumes of Dr. Eliot's Five-Foot Shelf you will perceive that all selections are preceded by an introductory critical essay. These you will find of the greatest interest for they call to your attention in a most fascinating and illuminating manner the chief facts in the life of the author and how he came to write that particular book. You are told of the writer's personal traits, his struggles and his triumphs which helped to mold his life and the contribution he has made to world literature.

This skilfully-written essay is a "critique" of the particular selection that follows, establishing its place in literature and estimating it in comparison with other works by the same author. Lastly it suggests why you—as a cultivated man or woman—should read it. You are told how much to believe of Cellini's famous, bragging Autobiography, why Sir Walter Scott was forced to write from morning to midnight, and, to give still another instance, the circumstances surrounding Samuel Johnson's bitterly ironic letter to one of the greatest nobles of England, Lord Chesterfield.

A Series of Skilfully-written Essays

In selections, such as the books of the Bible, you are told what is most important to look for in these classics. Full explanation is made of the contents of a piece and an appreciation of the beauty and power of the selection is generally given so that you may more readily perceive its merits. Comparisons are frequently made between one work and another. These are of untold assistance in giving you a broad view of a certain period or of allied forms of literature and science.

If you are making a study of any given subject, you will often find that the Introductory Lectures furnish you with information which you can obtain nowhere else. By their variety, their simplicity of statement, and their fullness of detail, these critical essays are amply fitted to supplement the selections, adding greatly to your interest, and will help you extract the greatest benefit from them. This is really having university instruction at home, and more than that, by the greatest teacher of one of the greatest universities.

The Footnotes

AN extraordinarily helpful feature to the reader are the voluminous
footnotes which appear throughout the entire set. Every one
of the 22,462 pages has been carefully edited so that reader and student
may obtain the most from their reading and extract the full meaning
from the text.

These footnotes include explanations of involved passages, cross
references, interesting sidelights and criticisms. They contain titles
of books for supplementary reading, phrases and passages translated
from their original foreign languages, definitions of words and terms,
brief accounts of the lives of famous people mentioned in the text,
pronunciations of strange words, and many other invaluable helps to
the reader.

Comprehensive and Highly Explanatory

They indicate differences of opinion, they review trends of thought
related to those in the subject matter, they point out errors of judgment in the light of present day thinking, they mention important
events which influenced contemporary writing, they show the bearing
one scientific or geographic discovery had on another, they reveal the
relations existing among different countries, schools, and religions.
They clear up obscure meanings in the works of the older writers not
readily intelligible in the present day.

These exhaustive footnotes throughout the entire fifty volumes,
enable the reader to gain a full and comprehensive knowledge of the
selection which he is reading. Thus, the great pieces of literature
which go to make up the Harvard Classics are rendered completely
enjoyable and understandable to everyone. In every respect the footnotes correspond to the detailed explanations and comments given
by university lecturers in their college courses.

In no other work will you find such diversified and useful information on so many subjects. These footnotes, complete in every detail,
were prepared by scholars who have made their life work the study
of this immortal literature. They are but another splendid feature
of the Harvard Classics.

The General Index

THIS main Index to the Five-Foot Shelf is as complete as the human mind can make it. It is the only volume of its kind in existence; over $50,000 and a year of expert work were spent upon it. It contains 76,000 references and gives instant access to the worth while books of every age that have been written on every subject. Here, in fact, is the exhaustive key to this vast storehouse of knowledge.

The Index is extremely easy to use. Page 116 of the fiftieth volume fully and clearly explains the way in which contents have been compiled. But even the perusal of this explanatory note is almost unnecessary, for the Index is arranged so simply that the reader will find no difficulty in finding what he wants.

To the busy man who wants information for a speech, an article, an advertisement, or an editorial, this Index renders a service that cannot be computed in terms of dollars and cents. Long days of search would not bring to hand the wealth of material that can be obtained in a few minutes through this source.

Cross-indexed as thoroughly as it is, there are few items that can possibly escape you. Certainly the sub-divisions of each topic will enable you to find instantly what you are looking for.

Realizing the worth of this great work of reference, Dean Evans, of the Chattanooga Law School, said, "The Index Volume is a marvel of excellence. By it one may easily trace the best thoughts of the wisest men on all topics of vital human interest running through the ages."

The Index to the First Lines

Particularly valuable is the Index to the First Lines of poems, songs, hymns and psalms appearing in all the volumes of the Harvard Classics. Very often you hear or remember the first line of a poem quoted and are unable to establish the title or the author. This Index gives you the means by which you can "place" the verse in your own mind.

If you yourself are hunting for an apt quotation, a line of poetry, or even the author, his dates of birth and death, or the title of his poem, you have only to look up the first line of poetry and be referred to the place where the author and his work are mentioned. By using this convenient list of first lines, you often save yourself hours of fruitless search and, in some cases, mental embarrassment at not being able to locate a well known poem. In this fashion does the Index to First Lines take the place of a private secretary.

The Chronological Index

Volume fifty contains a complete chronological index starting with the earliest known dates, centuries before Christ, and coming down to our present day. This index lists the years of birth and death of the world's famous men, with explanatory comments on each. It gives dates of industrial, social, and religious revolutions, of decisive battles, and when epoch-making speeches were delivered, on what dates classic dramas were written, acted, and published, and when notable scientific discoveries were made.

This Index may be used with Dr. Eliot's prescribed courses of reading, and will be invaluable for reference. It is difficult to estimate the importance of this specialized index to the student of history, civilization, literature and allied subjects. The entire story of mankind may be read from this table of dates.

The Readers' Guide

THE Readers' Guide offers you courses of reading and study of a broad educational nature. By following the suggested outline of any course which you will find in volume fifty, you will obtain a splendid working knowledge of that subject comparable in every way to that which you would receive in a university. These courses as laid out by Dr. Eliot are designed to afford a liberal, general training.

More than any other American educator, Dr. Eliot is responsible for our modern methods of university teaching. He inspired and formulated the educational system not only at Harvard, of which he was president for forty years, but he influenced the curriculums in schools and colleges throughout the country. These courses therefore in which he took so great an interest and care in outlining for reading in the Harvard Classics bear the stamp of the highest authority.

The Value of Selected Reading

Dr. Eliot was a staunch believer in systematized reading. He held that reading so done, would lead to a liberal education. Reading not so organized was of negative value. He felt that directed reading leading progressively through a subject from its simpler to its more complicated aspects was the best possible training. The reading courses in the Harvard Classics represent his idea of orderly, worth while reading for every man and woman.

Their value to the ambitious, serious student cannot be easily estimated. A faithful carrying out of the assignments in the outlines will give a very remarkable knowledge of the subjects studied.

Out of his wide experience, Dr. Eliot prescribes here eleven reading courses. These are all on cultural subjects which form the backbone of a liberal college education and they embrace such interesting and instructive topics as The History of Civilization, Religion and Philosophy, Education, Science, Politics, Voyages and Travels, Criticism of Literature and the Fine Arts, Drama, Biography and Letters, Essays, Narrative Poetry and Prose Fiction. In each of these widely diversified subjects, Dr. Eliot has arranged a broad, comprehensive reading list from the writings appearing in the Five-Foot Shelf and arranged them according to subject and the order in which they should be read. Logically, Dr. Eliot chooses the simpler selections first, which give the elemental or general survey of the subject and gradually proceeds to the more difficult aspects as the reader progresses.

A Comprehensive Study Course

But so wisely has the great educator selected his lists, that the topics for reading are also generally in chronological order. In this way you start at the beginning of man's thought on a subject and follow it down through the centuries. Dr. Eliot has also written a short description of each reading course, explaining its plan and purpose and telling you what is most important to get from your reading. He comments briefly on the classic selections and often mentions the chief facts in the lives of the famous authors. The short prefaces in fact, serve the same highly useful purpose as a professor's introductory remarks in a classroom.

In arranging these courses Dr. Eliot has mingled with the serious, in pleasant proportion, lighter pieces in order to give variety and entertainment, as well as instruction. These include novels reflecting the life of the times, witty poems, stirring ballads, and essays dealing appropriately with the subjects. Dr. Eliot's simple but thorough plan of study enables you to master his courses with the greatest benefit to yourself. This Readers' Guide is a valuable key which unlocks the knowledge, the wit and wisdom in the Harvard Classics. It is but another of the many precious contributions Dr. Eliot makes to the cause of real education.

It is not at all out of the way to suggest that he had a very definite reference to the reading courses when he made that famous statement about the Harvard Classics, that, "the faithful and considerate reading of these books will give any man the essentials of a liberal education even if he devote to them but fifteen minutes a day."

Selections for Boys and Girls
From Twelve to Eighteen Years of Age

PRESIDENT ELIOT in consultation with President Neilson of Smith College prepared a list of selections from the Harvard Classics suitable for the use of children ranging in age from twelve to eighteen years. There is no place where the Harvard Classics finds greater usefulness than to children. If you have children in your family—growing boys and girls—let them have free access to the Harvard Classics.

In order that the child may have a pleasant introduction to this monumental work, there are here given those pieces which the boy or girl can read and enjoy. Dr. Eliot has chosen more than sixty stories, poems and articles with the numbers of volumes and pages where they appear in the Five-Foot Shelf. Here will be found the world's best tales, plays and verses arranged in the order in which they are likely to appeal to growing children. The easier, simpler tales come first and give the younger members of the family a solid foundation of interesting, easily understood literature. As the children develop, they can follow down the list and read the more advanced selections. Thus, they have secured a grasp on worth while books and have developed a taste for reading which will ever be a constant source of pleasure and satisfaction.

They Create a Sound Cultural Background

The Harvard Classics bring the growing mind of the boy and girl in contact with the greatest reading of all time. These books will serve to whet their healthy and eager curiosity, for they are the finest writings of the greatest creative minds of the world. The Harvard Classics will bring to the growing boy and girl a familiarity with the supreme literature, at the impressionable age when cultural habits are formed for a lifetime.

These selections will train your children to turn to the Harvard Classics for their entertainment, stimulation and recreation, and they will use this great library throughout their school years.

The Lecture Volume

THE additional volume to the fifty volume set is entitled, "Lectures on the Harvard Classics." This extraordinary series falls into twelve main divisions of knowledge such as, History, Poetry, Natural Science, Philosophy, Biography, Prose Fiction, Criticism and the Essay, Education, Political Science, Drama, Voyages and Travel and Religion, with each division containing five lectures on those subjects. Thus there are sixty lectures in all. If you will turn to Dr. Eliot's short introduction, you will sense the importance he puts on this series of lectures in promoting the educational object he had in mind when he made the collection. Also turn to President Neilson's preface in which he says, the lectures open the door to the Harvard Classics "the great storehouse of standard works in all the main departments of intellectual activity."

By an Array of Famous Professors

Through these lectures, as Dr. Neilson further writes, the student is introduced to a vast range of topics under the guidance of distinguished professors. Among these are George Pierce Baker, probably the best known teacher today of the drama in America; Thomas Nixon Carver, the most noted authority on political science and economics in this country; Bliss Perry, famous professor at Harvard, editor and lecturer; Ralph Barton Perry, one of America's outstanding philosophers and many others equally prominent.

To have the privilege to hear this group of men speak or read their great lectures is an opportunity which cannot be measured in terms of dollars and cents. These lectures will do much to broaden your outlook and extend your interests to diversified, vital branches of thought. The footnotes, too, in this volume furnish splendid supplementary material for reading. They make the author's meaning perfectly clear to you and offer interesting information on the matter in the text. The value of this volume with the other features such as the Introduction, Notes, Guides to Reading and Indexes as Professor Neilson states, "may thus claim to constitute a reading course unparalleled in comprehensiveness and authority."

The Daily Reading Guide

PRESIDENT ELIOT wrote in his introduction to the Harvard Classics, "In my opinion, a five-foot shelf would hold books enough to give a liberal education to any one who would read them with devotion, even if he could spare but fifteen minutes a day for reading." With this very definitely in mind, we have prepared a daily reading guide in which the assignments chosen appropriately enough, will take the usual person about fifteen minutes to read with leisurely enjoyment. These selections assigned for each day in the year as you will see, are introduced by comments on the author, the subjects or the chief characters. They will serve to introduce you in the most pleasant manner possible to the Harvard Classics. They will enable you to browse enjoyably among the world's immortal writings with entertainment and stimulation in endless variety.

Form this Pleasant and Exhilarating Habit

To take a few minutes out of your busy day to commune with these great writers of all time is one of the finest habits possible. That fifteen minutes will carry you on wings of romance and adventure to other lands, to the scenes of other days and will break the monotony of your days, will change the course of your thinking, will give you the privilege of contact with the great minds whose writings have stimulated and inspired mankind over the centuries.

As comprehensive as it is, the Daily Reading Guide does not presume to exhaust the wealth of interest and profit that lies between the pages of this great library. We believe that once you have been afforded a taste of the delights of the imperishable writings you will straightway turn back to read the larger works to which you have been so pleasantly introduced. In addition to the Reading Guide, you have Dr. Eliot's Reading Courses as outlined in volume fifty— the remarkable course of sixty lectures and the index with its seventy-six thousand references, all of which will provide you with fascinating topics in an unfailing diversity. Thus the Harvard Classics afford you in generous measure entertainment and enchantment and intellectual stimulus.

JANUARY

St. Agnes' Eve!—Ah, bitter chill it was!
The owl, for all his feathers, was a-cold;
The hare limp'd trembling through the frozen grass,
And silent was the flock in woolly fold. . .

KEATS (Vol. 41, p. 883)

1 Franklin's Advice for the New Year

"Resolution: Resolve to perform what you ought; perform without fail what you resolve"—was one of the rules for success framed by America's first "self-made" man.

Read from FRANKLIN'S AUTOBIOGRAPHY.................Vol. 1, pp. 79-85

2 School-Day Poems of John Milton

At the age of sixteen, Milton first appeared before the public eye as a promising young poet. These early verses, written while he was a boy in school, indicate his brilliant future.

(First edition of Milton's collected poems published Jan. 2, 1645.)
Read: MILTON'S POEMS..............................Vol. 4, pp. 7-18

3 Cicero on Friendship

"Fire and water are not of more universal use than friendship"— such is the high value put upon this great human relationship by the most famous orator of Rome.

(Cicero born Jan. 3, 106 B. C.)
Read from Cicero ON FRIENDSHIP....................Vol. 9, pp. 16-26

4 A Flounder Fish Story

A fisherman, so the story goes, once caught a flounder that spoke, begging to be released. This was granted, whereupon the fisherman's wife demanded that it grant her one miracle after another, until even the flounder was disgusted.

(Jacob Grimm, elder of the famous Grimm brothers, born Jan. 4, 1785.)
Read from GRIMM'S FAIRY TALES....................Vol. 17, pp. 83-90

5 The Soaring Eagle and Contented Stork

Mazzini labored for the freedom of Italy, but was exiled. Byron and Goethe also battled for liberty. Mazzini wrote an essay in which he compared Byron to a soaring eagle and Goethe to a contented stork.

(Byron arrived in Greece to fight for Greek freedom, Jan. 5, 1824.)
Read: Mazzini's BYRON AND GOETHE...............Vol. 32, pp. 377-396

JANUARY *Reading Guide*

6 Warned by Hector's Ghost

In the dead of night Hector's ghost appeared to warn Æneas of the impending doom to come upon the walled city of Troy. Æneas lifted his aged father on his back and, taking his son by the hand, sought safety in flight. Off to Latium!

(*H. Schliemann, discoverer of ancient Troy, born Jan. 6, 1822.*)
Read from Virgil's ÆNEID........................Vol. 13, pp. 109-127

7 If He Yawned, She Lost Her Head!

The Sultan had a habit of beheading each dawn his beautiful bride of the night before, until he encountered Scheherazade. Cleverly she saved her life a thousand and one mornings.

Read from THE THOUSAND AND ONE NIGHTS...........Vol. 16, pp. 5-13

8 Trying the Patience of Job

God was pleased with the piety of Job, but Satan accredited the piety to Job's prosperity and happiness. So a trial was made. See how each succeeding affliction visited on Job shook the depths of his nature, and how he survived.

Read from THE BOOK OF JOB........................Vol. 44, pp. 71-87

9 A Treasure Hunt in Nombre de Dios

With only fifty-two men, Sir Francis Drake conceives the idea of attacking his archenemy, Spain, at her most vulnerable point the treasure at Nombre de Dios.

(*Drake died at Nombre de Dios, Jan. 9, 1596.*)
Read from Nichol's SIR FRANCIS DRAKE REVIVED......Vol. 33, pp. 135-145

10 Where Love Lies Waiting

King Pantheus of Thebes contended against Dionysus, the God, for the adoration of the Theban women. The god was winning by bewitching the women when the king interceded. Euripides tells the story in a masterpiece of Greek drama.

Read from Euripides' THE BACCHAE.................Vol. 8, pp. 368-372

11 Hamilton—Father of Wall Street

Hamilton organized the Treasury Department. He penned most of the Federalist papers, which were greatly influential in bringing New York into the Union—the first step toward its eminent position in national and world finance.

(*Alexander Hamilton born Jan. 11, 1757.*)
Read: THE FEDERALIST...........................Vol. 43, pp. 199-207

January *Reading Guide*

12 **What Is Good Taste?**

A Turkish sultan, relates Burke, when shown a picture of the beheaded John the Baptist, praised many things, but pointed out one gruesome defect. Did this observation show the sultan to be an inferior judge of art?

(Edmund Burke born Jan. 12, 1729.)
Read: Burke On Taste...........................Vol. 24, pp. 11-26

13 **Rousseau Seeks Sanctuary in England**

Rousseau taught that men were not created free and equal. To substantiate his daring beliefs he traced man's history back to his primitive beginnings. For his teachings, Rousseau was forced to seek refuge in England.

(Jean Jacques Rousseau arrived in England, Jan. 13, 1766.)
Read from Rousseau's Inquiry on Inequality........Vol. 34, pp. 215-228

14 **The First Step Toward Independence**

(Fundamental Orders of Connecticut adopted Jan. 14, 1639.)
The Fundamental Orders of Connecticut is "the first written constitution as a permanent limitation on governmental power, known in history." It is the work of the Connecticut Yankee.

Read: The Fundamental Orders of Connecticut.....Vol. 43, pp. 60-65

15 **"The Moving Finger Writes"**

("Rubaiyat of Omar Khayyam" first published Jan. 15, 1859.)
Omar Khayyam laughed and enjoyed the good things of life. His "Rubaiyat," the most popular philosophic poem, is the best of all books to dip into for an alluring thought.

Read from The Rubaiyat of Omar Khayyam.......Vol. 41, pp. 943-953

16 **The Old Woman and the Wine Jar**

An old woman once found a wine jar, but it was empty. She sniffed at the mouth of the jar and said: "What memories cling 'round the instruments of our pleasure."

Read from Æsop's Fables.............Vol. 17, pp. 43-44; also pp. 31-43

17 **Franklin's Family Tree**

(Benjamin Franklin born Jan. 17, 1706.)
Good middle-class people, Franklin boasts, were his ancestors. Some have attributed his genius to his being the youngest son of the youngest son for five generations. In his famous autobiography, he reveals quaint family history.

Read from Franklin's Autobiography.................Vol. 1, pp. 5-15

JANUARY *Reading Guide*

18 Origin of Yale "Brekekekex-Ko-ax"

"Shall I crack any of those old jokes, master, at which the audience never fails to laugh?" Like an up-to-date vaudeville team, Xanthias and Dionysus start off a dialogue that mingles wit and poetry with humor and keen satire.

Read from Aristophanes' THE FROGS.................Vol. 8, pp. 439-449

19 Poe on Poetry

Regarded in Europe as one of America's greatest writers, Poe originated the detective story, perfected the mystery short story, and produced America's first great poems. Here he unravels the fabric of which all poetry is woven.

(*Edgar Allan Poe born Jan. 19, 1809.*)

Read from Poe's THE POETIC PRINCIPLE.............Vol. 28, pp. 371-380

20 "Ah! It Is St. Agnes' Eve—"

(*St. Agnes' Eve, Jan. 20.*)

At midnight on the eve of St. Agnes there were certain solemn ceremonies which all virgins must perform to have "visions of delight and soft adorings from their loves." Porphyro took advantage of this custom to win his bride.

Read: Keats' EVE OF ST. AGNES...................Vol. 41, pp. 883-893

21 The Nightingale's Healing Melody

The Emperor of China lies on his deathbed grieving for the song of his favorite bird. Hark, the song! It charms, coaxes, and bribes Death to depart. It brings new life to the master.

Read from ANDERSEN'S TALES.....................Vol. 17, pp. 301-310

22 A King's Pleasure Now Yours

The classic plays of French literature are produced to-day precisely as when they were given for the resplendent kings they were written to please. We are fortunate to have in English, excellent translations of these noble plays.

(*Corneille elected to French Academy, Jan. 22, 1647.*)

Read from Corneille's POLYEUCTE.....................Vol. 26, pp. 77-87

23 Pascal Knew Men and Triangles

(*Pascal publishes "Provincial Letters," Jan. 23, 1656.*)

Pascal, the keen-minded philosopher and mathematician, fathomed the human traits of man's nature with the same accurate measurements which made him famous in the realm of geometry. Read his searching analysis of man's conceit.

Read: Pascal's THE ART OF PERSUASION.............Vol. 48, pp. 400-411

JANUARY *Reading Guide*

24 Odysseus Silenced the Sirens

When his ship approached the siren's rock, Odysseus stuffed
the ears of his crew with wax and had himself bound to the mast
that he might hear the alluring voice of the siren and yet not
wreck his ship on the enchanted rock.

Read from Homer's ODYSSEY......................Vol. 22, pp. 165-173

25 A Field Mouse Made Famous

A humble Scotchman, plowing his fields, turns over the nest of
a frightened mouse. He apologizes with the deepest sincerity
and explains how "the best-laid schemes o' mice an' men gang
aft agley."

(*Robert Burns born Jan. 25, 1759.*)
Read: To A MOUSE and Burns' other poems....Vol. 6, pp. 119-120, 388-394

26 In the Cradle of Civilization

A king who entombed his daughter in a golden cow—the worship of the bull and the cat—scandal of the court and the gossip
of the temples is given by Herodotus in his delightful story of
old Egypt.

Read from Herodotus' AN ACCOUNT OF EGYPT........Vol. 33, pp. 65-75

27 Dante and Beatrice in Paradise

Dante fell madly in love with Beatrice at first sight; but it is
doubted if he ever spoke to her in this world. He tells of his
happy meeting with Beatrice in Paradise.

(*Dante victim of political persecution in Florence, Jan. 27, 1302.*)
Read from Dante's DIVINE COMEDY................Vol. 20, pp. 267-279

28 Man's Wings

A pure heart, says Thomas à Kempis, comprehends the very
depths of Heaven and Hell. And it is by the wings of simplicity
and purity that man is lifted above all earthly things.

Read from Thomas à Kempis......................Vol. 7, pp. 242-249

29 Visits the Land of Fire

South of Patagonia is Tierra del Fuego—"The Land of Fire."
The natives of that primitive country are to-day almost extinct.
Darwin made a careful and vitally interesting study of that land
and its ill-fated inhabitants.

(*Darwin married Emma Wedgewood, Jan. 29, 1839.*)
Read from Darwin's VOYAGE OF THE BEAGLE.............Vol. 29, 209-221

January *Reading Guide*

30 **First Problem Play Popular**

Antigone, an orphan princess, defies a king's mandate and risks her life to do her duty to her brother. What is this duty which her brother calls her to perform and the king forbids?

(Sophocles died at Athens, Jan. 30, 405 B. C.)

Read from Sophocles' ANTIGONE.....................Vol. 8, pp. 255-266

31 **What "Don Quixote" Really Slew**

Slayer of windmills, rescuer of fair damsels in distress, eccentric Don Quixote, scores of years behind his time, set out on a mad quest of knight-errantry. Worlds of fun and killing satire are in this absorbing story of Cervantes.

Read from DON QUIXOTE...........................Vol. 14, pp. 60-67

Don Quixote, the ambitious amateur knight, was well ridiculed for his pains. (See Reading Assignment for January 31st.)

A FEW BOOKS ARE BETTER THAN MANY, AND A LITTLE TIME GIVEN TO A FAITHFUL STUDY OF THE FEW WILL BE ENOUGH TO QUICKEN THOUGHT AND ENRICH THE MIND.—CHANNING.

FEBRUARY

. . . howling Winter fled afar
To hills that prop the polar star;
And loves on deer-borne car to ride
With barren darkness at his side . . .
. . . sullen Winter! hear my prayer,
And gently rule the ruin'd year . . .

CAMPBELL (Vol. 41, p. 772)

1 King Arthur's Knights Find Holy Grail

The intrepid Knights of the Round Table were startled by "crackling and crying of thunder" which rang through the great hall of the castle. Then there entered "The Holy Grail covered with white samite."
Read from Malory's THE HOLY GRAIL.............Vol. 35, pp. 112-123

2 "Apparel Oft Proclaims the Man"

Before his son, Laertes, departs for a foreign country, Polonius advises him as to his conduct and dress, while Hamlet, the king's son, has to learn by experience.
(Shakespeare's twins—Hamnet and Judith—baptized Feb. 2, 1585.)
Read from Shakespeare's HAMLET.................Vol. 46, pp. 107-120

3 A House of Mirth and Revelry

While the cat's away the mice will play. Boisterous and ludicrous happenings occur in a house left in charge of a servant. But in midst of merriment the master returns.
(Ben Jonson receives life pension from James I, Feb. 3, 1619.)
Read from Jonson's THE ALCHEMIST................Vol. 47, pp. 543-558

4 "Genius, a Secret to Itself"

Thus wrote Carlyle, who affirms that great minds are unconscious of their stupendous strength. And each of us has his own peculiar mental attributes.
(Thomas Carlyle died Feb. 4, 1881.)
Read from Carlyle's CHARACTERISTICS.............Vol. 25, pp. 319-327

5 Diamonds, Diamonds Everywhere!

Trapped in a valley filled with huge diamonds guarded by venomous serpents, Sindibad devised a clever means of escaping with many of the glittering jewels.
Read from THE THOUSAND AND ONE NIGHTS..........Vol. 16, pp. 243-250

FEBRUARY *Reading Guide*

6 **Charles Lamb Suggests To-day's Reading**

"The reluctant pangs of abdicating royalty in 'Edward' furnished hints which Shakespeare scarcely improved in his 'Richard the Second,' and the death scene of Marlowe's King moves to pity and terror."—CHARLES LAMB.

(Christopher Marlowe born Feb. 6, 1564.)
Read from Marlowe's EDWARD THE SECOND . . . . Vol. 46, pp. 73-89

7 **A Letter from a Lion**

Johnson was not always a conventional guest. Graciously treated, he responded in like manner, but offended, Johnson could wield a pen dripping with vitriol.

(Samuel Johnson writes to Lord Chesterfield, Feb. 7, 1755.)
Read: LETTER TO LORD CHESTERFIELD . . . . Vol. 39, pp. 206-207

8 **Tragic Death of a World-Famous Beauty**

"But I, the Queen of a' Scotland, maun lie in prison strang." Burns sings of poor Mary bound by chains, yearning for the day when flowers would "bloom on her peaceful grave."

(Mary, Queen of Scots, beheaded Feb. 8, 1587.)
Read from BURNS' POEMS . . . . Vol. 6, pp. 396-406

9 **Rest Between Wars**

Tacitus, the historian, visited the virile German tribes in their primitive homes on the banks of the Rhine. He was surprised to learn that the men so active and eager in war lolled in indolence during the intervals between.

Read from Tacitus ON GERMANY . . . . Vol. 33, pp. 93-102

10 **No Fancy for a Plain Gentleman**

Voltaire once visited Congreve. This famous dramatist requested to be regarded only as a plain gentleman. "Had you been that I should never have come to see you," Voltaire cynically replies.

(William Congreve baptized Feb. 10, 1670.)
Read from Voltaire's LETTERS ON THE ENGLISH . . . . Vol. 34, pp. 130-140

11 **The Queen Freezes Her Philosophy**

Descartes was slain through the eccentric whim of a queen who demanded that he tutor her in the freezing dawn in the dead of winter. His philosophy lives in this essay.

(René Descartes died at Stockholm, Feb. 11, 1650.)
Read from Descartes' DISCOURSE ON METHOD . . . . Vol. 34, pp. 5-20

February *Reading Guide*

12 **Oxford Corrects Lincoln's Mistake**

Lincoln himself thought his famous Gettysburg Address was a failure. To-day the whole world acclaims its greatness. Cast in bronze, it hangs on the wall of Balliol College, Oxford, regarded as the perfection of English prose.

(Abraham Lincoln born Feb. 12, 1809.)

Read: LINCOLN'S WRITINGS........................Vol. 43, pp. 415-420

13 **The Frank Story of an Amazing Life**

At the age of fifty-eight Benvenuto Cellini shaved his head and retired to a monastery to write his own story of murder, passion, and great deeds of the Renaissance. His life is a vivid picture of the most colorful period in history, a period when statecraft and religion and black magic and assassination were naïvely mingled in men's lives.

(Benvenuto Cellini died Feb. 13, 1570.)

Read from CELLINI'S AUTOBIOGRAPHY.................Vol. 31, pp. 68-80

14 **Love Always Young**

(St. Valentine's Day.)

Pascal—an original genius—purposed to master everything that was new in art and science. He was a mathematician and scientist as well as a religious enthusiast and moralist, and he shows a decidedly human side of his nature in this superb essay on Love.

Read: Pascal's DISCOURSE ON THE PASSION OF LOVE....Vol. 48, pp. 411-421

15 **The World Well Lost?**

The romantic and heedless loves of Antony and Cleopatra figure prominently in history, literature, and drama. Dryden made a fascinating play from the story of Antony, who sacrificed the leadership of Rome, reputation, and life itself for love of the Egyptian queen, who followed him in death.

(Mark Antony offers Cæsar crown at Rome, Feb. 15, 44 B. C.)

Read from Dryden's ALL FOR LOVE..................Vol. 18, pp. 53-69

16 **Social Circles Among Ants**

Ants have slaves who work for them. These slaves make the nests, feed the master ants, tend the eggs, and do the moving when a colony of ants migrate. Darwin minutely describes the habits and lives of the industrious ants and their marvelous social organization—a wonder to mankind.

Read from Darwin's ORIGIN OF SPECIES.............Vol. 11, pp. 264-268

FEBRUARY *Reading Guide*

17 Death His Curtain Call

While acting in one of his own plays, Molière was suddenly stricken and died shortly after the final curtain. He took an important rôle in "Tartuffe" which introduces to literature a character as famous as Shakespeare's Falstaff.

(Molière died Feb. 17, 1673.)

Read from Molière's TARTUFFE....................Vol. 26, pp. 199-217

18 Lasting Peace with Great Britain

All Americans should know this treaty which finally inaugurated an era of peace and good understanding with England. For over a hundred years this peace has been unbroken.

(Treaty with Great Britain proclaimed Feb. 18, 1815.)

Read: TREATY WITH GREAT BRITAIN (1814)..........Vol. 43, pp. 255-264

19 Earthly Experience of a Chinese Goddess

The thousandth celestial wife of the Garland God slipped and fell to earth, where she took mortal form and served as an attendant in a temple. Death finally released her and she went back to heaven to tell her lord of the ways of men.

Read from the BUDDHIST WRITINGS.................Vol. 45, pp. 693-701

20 Voltaire Observes the Quakers

Because the early Quakers shook, trembled, and quaked when they became inspired—they received the title of "Quakers." This sect attracted the keen-minded Voltaire, who made interesting notes on them during his visit to England.

Read from Voltaire's LETTERS ON THE ENGLISH........Vol. 34, pp. 65-78

21 Does Football Make a College?

Just what makes a university? A group of fine buildings? A library? A staff of well-trained teachers? A body of eager students? A winning football team? Cardinal Newman defines the prime functions of a university.

(Cardinal Newman born Feb. 21, 1801.)

Read from Newman's THE IDEA OF A UNIVERSITY........Vol. 28, pp. 31-39

22 An Ode for Washington's Birthday

(George Washington born Feb. 22, 1732.)

Burns asks for Columbia's harp, and then sings of liberty. He bewails the sad state of the land of Alfred and Wallace which once championed liberty, and now fights for tyranny.

Read from BURNS' POEMS........................Vol. 6, pp. 492-494

FEBRUARY *Reading Guide*

23   Pepys' Nose for News

Gossipy, witty Pepys had a curiosity that made him famous. He knew all the news of court and street. Stevenson, who never put his pen to a dull subject, writes of Pepys.

(Samuel Pepys born Feb. 23, 1632.)

Read from Stevenson's SAMUEL PEPYS..............Vol. 28, pp. 285-292

24   Lights and Shadows of Milton

In a superb poem, Milton bids Loathed Melancholy begone to some dark cell. He calls for the joys of youth and vows eternal faith with them.

(John Milton marries his third wife, Elizabeth Marshall, Feb. 24, 1662.)

Read: MILTON'S POEMS..............................Vol. 4, pp. 30-38

25   Punished for Too Sharp a Wit

The brilliant wit and cutting satire of Defoe made for him friends and enemies—but mostly enemies. So piercing and two-edged was "The Shortest-Way with Dissenters" that he was fined, imprisoned and pilloried.

("The Shortest-Way with Dissenters" censored, Feb. 25, 1703.)

Read: THE SHORTEST-WAY WITH DISSENTERS.........Vol. 27, pp. 133-147

26   A David Who Side-stepped Goliath

Hugo was insulted by the most powerful critics in France. He put into the preface of a play "his sling and his stone" by which others might slay "the classical Goliath."

(Victor Hugo born Feb. 26, 1802.)

Read: HUGO'S PREFACE TO CROMWELL................Vol. 39, pp. 337-349

27   Poet Apostle of Good Cheer

(Longfellow born Feb. 27, 1807.)

"Tell me not in mournful numbers, life is but an empty dream . . ."
"Stars of the summer night! Far in yon azure deeps—"
So begin poems that have charmed and cheered thousands.

Read from LONGFELLOW'S POEMS.................Vol. 42, pp. 1264-1280

28   Spoke Latin First

(Michel de Montaigne born Feb. 28, 1533.)

Proficient in Latin even before he knew his own tongue, Montaigne received an unusual education. His whole life was spent in storing up his choice thoughts for our profit and pleasure.

Read from Montaigne's ESSAYS.....................Vol. 32, pp. 29-40

FEBRUARY *Reading Guide*

LEAP YEAR

29 **Goethe's Tale of a Maiden in Love**

To either Saint Patrick or the Scottish Parliament of 1228 go the honors—or dishonors—of originating the traditions attending this day; says the latter, *"ilka maiden ladee, of baith high and lowe estait, shall hae libertie to speak ye man she likes."* The course of true love runs smooth in Goethe's narrative poem, enduring today for its characterization and swift-flowing lines.

Begin HERMANN AND DOROTHEA . . . . Vol. 19, p. 337; also pp. 395-410

Dr. William Harvey established the fact that the arteries carry blood by feeling his own pulse while in a hot bath. (See Reading Assignment for June 3rd.)

A BLESSED COMPANION IS A BOOK,—A BOOK THAT FITLY CHOSEN IS A LIFE-LONG FRIEND.—DOUGLAS JERROULD.

MARCH

Old Winter back to the savage hills
Withdraweth his force, decrepid now.

GOETHE (Vol. 19, p. 43)

1 Invented Sir Roger de Coverly

Word pictures are often more vivid than photographs. Steele had a gift for originating characters that are remembered longer than flesh and blood people. Sir Roger de Coverly and Will Honeycomb are now bold figures in literature.

(First issue of the "Spectator," published March 1, 1711.)
Read: THE SPECTATOR CLUB.........................Vol. 27, pp. 83-87

2 What Sailors Do on Sunday

"A sailor's liberty is but for a day," as Dana explains. Dressed in his Sunday best, the sailor feels like a dashing Beau Brummel; and sets out to enjoy his freedom. "While it lasts it is perfect. He is under no one's eye and can do whatever he pleases."

Read from Dana's TWO YEARS BEFORE THE MAST......Vol. 23, pp. 112-119

3 For Poets and Fishermen

Isaak Walton, famed patron of fishermen, appreciated other arts and hobbies. He writes of George Herbert, a preacher whose hobby was poetry.

(George Herbert died March 3, 1633.)
Read from Walton's LIFE OF GEORGE HERBERT......Vol. 15, pp. 373-382

4 Penn—Pioneer, Thinker, and Builder

(King Charles grants Penn charter of Pennsylvania, March 4, 1681.)
Penn, true to Quaker beliefs, came before the king with his hat on. The king overlooked this and later made him governor of Pennsylvania. A sagacious Penn is revealed in his writings.

Read from Penn's SOME FRUITS OF SOLITUDE.........Vol. 1, pp. 321-330

5 Laughed at Locks

Prison walls were the least of Cellini's troubles. "Lock me well up and watch me, for I shall certainly contrive to escape." In spite of this warning, the utmost care of the jailers only furnished amusement for the dauntless Cellini.

Read from CELLINI'S AUTOBIOGRAPHY..............Vol. 31, pp. 214-224

March *Reading Guide*

6 West Point's Outcast, America's First Great Poet
(Poe expelled from West Point, March 6, 1831.)
Edgar Allan Poe was expelled from West Point and disinherited.
So poor was he that when his young wife lay dying, he could
not afford a fire to warm her. The weirdness and despair of
"The Raven" is particularly symbolic of his life.
Read: Poe's THE RAVEN........................Vol. 42, pp. 1227-1230

7 Bacon Warns Judges
Bacon pointed out that a judge's duty was to interpret laws and
not to make laws. This single essay of Bacon's is a richly con-
densed summary of the ethics of law.
(Bacon made Keeper of the Great Seal of England, March 7, 1616.)
Read: Bacon OF JUDICATURE........................Vol. 3, pp. 130-134

8 Dangerous Experiment with a Wife
Anselmo and Lothario were close friends. Anselmo, anxious to
learn if his wife were perfect, as he believed her to be, makes
an unusual proposal to his old friend.
Read from Cervantes' DON QUIXOTE...............Vol. 14, pp. 307-319

9 Common Sense and Good Manners
Swift regretted the laws against dueling because dueling at least
was a good means of ridding the country of bores and fools.
His keen eye penetrated social customs and saw the common
sense that governed good manners.
(Passage of laws against dueling in England, March 9, 1679.)
Read: TREATISE ON GOOD MANNERS..................Vol. 27, pp. 99-103

10 Beaumont—The Adonis of Elizabethan Playwrights
In the days when contact with the theatre meant exile from the
best society, Beaumont and Fletcher, men from good families,
dared to ally themselves with the stage as playwrights. "Philaster" won them immortal praise.
Read from PHILASTER............................Vol. 47, pp. 667-677

11 Gain Gleaned from Suffering
We are paid for our suffering and we pay for our happiness.
Every ache, every sorrow receives its recompense here on earth.
Emerson gives the basis for this conviction.
(Emerson ordained Unitarian minister, March 11, 1829.)
Read from Emerson's COMPENSATION..................Vol. 5, pp. 85-92

MARCH *Reading Guide*

12 An Irish Bishop's Wit

Berkeley believed in a great religious future for America. He lived three years in Rhode Island, and made plans for a college in Bermuda.

(Bishop Berkeley born March 12, 1685.)
Read from Berkeley's THREE DIALOGUES...........Vol. 37, pp. 228-238

13 Before Nobility Ran Tea Rooms

Manzoni has pictured in this thrilling romance of the seventeenth century nobility, the pompous and sporting life of those good old days when nobles lived sumptuously in spacious castles surrounded by vast estates.

Read from Manzoni's I PROMESSI SPOSI.............Vol. 21, pp. 318-332

14 A Maiden's Forfeit

"This gentlewoman that ye lead with you is a maid?" demanded the knight. "Sir," said she, "a maid I am." "Then she must yield us the custom of this castle."

(Malory, recorder of King Arthur stories, died March 14, 1470.)
Read from THE HOLY GRAIL......................Vol. 35, pp. 194-200

15 Beware the Ides of March!

(Ides of March, March 15.)
Twice warned of the danger that threatened him on the Ides of March, although "the earth rocked and the stars fell and headless men walked in the Forum," Cæsar goes to the doom awaiting him in the Senate Chamber.

Read from Plutarch's CÆSAR......................Vol. 12, pp. 315-321

16 Crabs Climb Trees?

Many amazing things happen in the Malay jungles. For example, Darwin tells about a crab that climbs trees and walks down the trunks for an occasional bath in a pool.

Read from Darwin's VOYAGE OF THE BEAGLE........Vol. 29, pp. 466-475

17 An Old Irish Legend

(St. Patrick's Day.)
An old Irish legend tells how, while St. Patrick was preaching about Paradise and Hell, several of his audience begged to be allowed to investigate the reality of these places. St. Patrick actually satisfied their curiosity.

Read from THE POETRY OF THE CELTIC RACES........Vol. 32, pp. 174-182

March *Reading Guide*

18 New Way to Pay Old Debts

A cunning uncle cheats his worthless nephew out of his fortune. The nephew, laughing stock of his former servants, sets out to retrieve his old position and riches.

(Massinger buried March 18, 1640.)

Read from A NEW WAY TO PAY OLD DEBTS.........Vol. 47, pp. 859-870

19 Seeing Old Egypt

The mysterious Egyptian temples, the floating islands, the huge pyramids and the many wonders of ancient Egypt are pictured for you by Herodotus.

(Last recorded event in Herodotus' history dated March 19, 478 B. C.)

Read from Herodotus' AN ACCOUNT OF EGYPT.........Vol. 33, pp. 72-84

20 Apples, Feathers, and Coals

Sir Isaac Newton was aided in his momentous discoveries by the most insignificant objects—even apples, feathers, and coal. Voltaire discusses the wondrous discoveries of Newton.

(Sir Isaac Newton died March 20, 1727.)

Read from Voltaire's LETTERS ON THE ENGLISH.......Vol. 34, pp. 113-124

21 1,000 Years of History on the Surface of a Shield

Venus, mother of Æneas and wife of Vulcan, obtained from her husband, by seductive witchery, a marvelous shield whose surface reflected a thousand years of future events. Venus describes the wonders of the magic armor.

Read from Virgil's ÆNEID.........................Vol. 13, pp. 280-292

22 From Puppet Show to Majestic Drama

The Faust legend, which can be traced to puppet shows of earlier days, portrays a philosopher who, through Satan's aid and in return for the price of his soul, works magic at will. From this rude framework Goethe has reared a drama of sublime grandeur.

(Goethe died March 22, 1832.)

Read from Goethe's FAUST.........................Vol. 19, pp. 23-36

23 First of a Thousand Harem Stories

Shahrazad, favorite of the treacherous Sultan's harem, selected a most thrilling story for her bridal night. By leaving it unfinished she was privileged to live to continue it the next night—and so on for a thousand and one nights.

Read from THE THOUSAND AND ONE NIGHTS...........Vol. 16, pp. 15-24

MARCH *Reading Guide*

24 A Queen Pleads

Guenevere, King Arthur's queen, justly accused but harshly treated, makes a noble and brave attempt to convince her court that Gawaine lied and that Launcelot was true.

(William Morris born March 24, 1834.)
Read: Morris' DEFENSE OF GUENEVERE............Vol. 42, pp. 1183-1193

25 How Conscience Makes Cowards of Us All

Hamlet pondered over which course contained the least unhappiness—whether to suffer here and not incur new dangers, or whether to end it all and chance the unknown terrors of the next world. See how Hamlet reasoned.

(Shakespeare makes his will, March 25, 1616.)
Read from Shakespeare's HAMLET.................Vol. 46, pp. 144-158

26 "2,500 Years Ago Æsop Said . . ."

Men in all ages have recognized the ingenuity of the practical philosophy and freshness of Æsop's allegories. Spend a few delightful moments with the wit and wisdom of Æsop.

(Caxton prints Æsop's Fables, March 26, 1484.)
Read from ÆSOP's FABLES........................Vol. 17, pp. 21-30

27 When Is a Lie Not a Lie?

Is lying or quibbling ever permissible? May one juggle words so a truth is conveyed through a lie and a lie told by a truth? Stevenson unravels this puzzle.

Read: Stevenson's TRUTH OF INTERCOURSE..........Vol. 28, pp. 277-284

28 Pins and Other Points

The making of a simple pin is one of the most complex affairs of modern industry. Adam Smith regards the process from the worker's point of view, and shows the many and varied economic principles that are involved in pin making.

Read from Adam Smith's WEALTH OF NATIONS.........Vol. 10, pp. 9-17

29 Hero and Goddess Break Engagement

Brynhild, favorite goddess of Norse mythology, plighted troth with Sigurd, fearless warrior. But Sigurd forgot Brynhild and married Gudrun, whose brother, Gunner, then set out to win the beautiful Brynhild. Complications very like a modern triangle arose.

Read from EPIC AND SAGA........................Vol. 49, pp. 307-317

March *Reading Guide*

30 **The Plague of Milan**

"I Promessi Sposi," a seventeenth century novel, vividly describes the devastating plague of Milan. Then whole families sickened in a few hours and died in less than a day's time of strange and violent complaints whose symptoms were unknown to physicians.

(*Capuchin monks given charge of the plague hospital in Milan, March 30, 1630.*)

Read from Manzoni's I PROMESSI SPOSI..............Vol. 21, pp. 500-512

31 **The Ghastly Whim of John Donne**

Monuments are usually made from death masks, but John Donne took pleasure in posing for his, wrapped from head to foot in a shroud. Isaak Walton tells of this in his fascinating biography of the eccentric poet.

(*John Donne died March 31, 1631.*)

Read from Walton's LIFE OF DR. DONNE............Vol. 15, pp. 364-369

Sir Francis Bacon believed that "the supreme law of all is the weal of the people." (See Reading Assignment for March 7th.)

IT WAS TRULY SAID, *OPTIMI CONSILIARII MORTUI* . . .
BOOKS WILL SPEAK PLAIN WHEN COUNSELLORS BLANCH.

—FRANCIS BACON.

APRIL

. . . proud-pied April, dress'd in all his trim,
Hath put a spirit of youth in everything,
That heavy Saturn laughed and leaped with him.

SHAKESPEARE (Vol. 40, p. 278)

1 **"Oh! to Be in England Now That April's There"**
Everyone knows the pangs of homesickness in the spring. Even bright, sparkling Italy could not wean Browning's affection from the green hedgerows of misty England.
Read: BROWNING'S POEMS......................Vol. 42, pp. 1068-1074

2 **A Spoon Dances in the Moonlight**
A huge spoon dressed in human finery, placed on a grave, appears to become convulsed when the moon's rays fall on it and dances to the tune of chanting natives. Weird sights, according to Darwin, abound in the South Seas.
Read from Darwin's VOYAGE OF THE BEAGLE........Vol. 29, pp. 462-471

3 **Romance with a Happy Ending**
"As a conqueror enters a surprised city; love made such resolutions as neither party was able to resist. She changed her name into Herbert the third day after this first interview."
(George Herbert born April 3, 1593.)
Read from Walton's LIFE OF GEORGE HERBERT.......Vol. 15, pp. 392-404

4 **The Mistakes of a Night**
Genial and rollicking fun are provided in this highly entertaining story of a man who mistakes a private house for an inn, and who treats his host's daughter like a serving maid.
(Oliver Goldsmith born April 4, 1774.)
Read from SHE STOOPS TO CONQUER.................Vol. 18, pp. 205-215

5 **You and Your Dreams**
Dreams and their causes interested Hobbes. Without superstition, the philosopher weighed the evidence of ghosts, goblins, and witches.
(Hobbes born April 5, 1588.)
Read from Hobbes' LEVIATHAN....................Vol. 34, pp. 313-322

APRIL *Reading Guide*

6 Who Is Bad?

Badness has many interpretations, a different definition has been the dictate of each new generation. The solution of the eternal riddle was earnestly sought by Marcus Aurelius.

(Marcus Aurelius born April 6, 121 A. D.)
Read: MARCUS AURELIUS' MEDITATIONS..............Vol. 2, pp. 243-253

7 Nature Guided His Pen

Wordsworth was so closely in touch with Nature that the simple beauty of flowers, woods, and fields is reflected in his poems as if Nature herself took up the pen and wrote.

(Wordsworth born April 7, 1770.)
Read: WORDSWORTH'S POEMS.......................Vol. 41, pp. 639-651

8 Beware the Vengeful Hounds!

Orestes, holding an avenging sword over his mother, is told: "Beware thy mother's vengeful hounds." How he pays for disregarding his mother's warning is told in this drama where a mother is slain to avenge a father's ghost.

Read from Æschylus' THE LIBATION BEARERS.........Vol. 8, pp. 111-121

9 A Perfect Land in a Wilderness of Waters

West of Peru there was reported to be a land where Truth and Science were used to promote the happiness and freedom of man. Here is Bacon's description of this ideal commonwealth.

(Francis Bacon died April 9, 1629.)
Read from Bacon's NEW ATLANTIS..................Vol. 3, pp. 145-155

10 Americans—by Will of the King

Before English adventurers could attempt settlement in America it was necessary first to get permission from the King. The charter of King James to the oldest American colony is an extremely important historical document.

(King James grants charter to Virginia, April 10, 1606.)
Read: FIRST CHARTER OF VIRGINIA...................Vol. 43, pp. 49-58

11 Danger in Being Young and Fair

The virgin beauty of Margaret enchanted Faust, who dazzled her with the brilliance of many gems. Margaret innocently took his gifts, believing that beauty should not "blush unseen"—but unmindful of consequences to follow.

Read from Goethe's FAUST.......................Vol. 19, pp. 115-131

APRIL *Reading Guide*

12 **The Perfect Argument**

You would doubtless like to know how to hold your own in any argument. Read what Leslie Stephen declares the finest specimen in our language of the conduct of argument.

Read from Berkeley's THREE DIALOGUES............Vol. 37, pp. 230-240

13 **Michelangelo His Boon Companion**

Kings, emperors, the greatest artists and sculptors of the Renaissance at its most magnificent period, walk through the pages of his autobiography—not as cold, austere, historical characters but as the intimate friends of Cellini.

Read from CELLINI's AUTOBIOGRAPHY................Vol. 31, pp. 23-35

14 **A Raid on Spanish Treasure in America**

Spanish towns in the New World were rich in treasure and tempting booty for English soldiers of fortune, who were venturesome and merciless. "Ho! for the Spanish Main!" was the rallying cry for all freebooters and buccaneers.

Read from Biggs' DRAKE'S GREAT ARMADA..........Vol. 33, pp. 229-242

15 **O Captain! My Captain!**

(*Lincoln died April 15, 1865.*)

The rugged, genuine Lincoln was idealized by Walt Whitman— the founder of the new school of American poetry. Two of Whitman's finest poems were inspired by Lincoln.

Read: WHITMAN'S POEMS......................Vol. 42, pp. 1412-1420

16 **Inside the Gates of Hell**

The city of Dis, within the gates of Hell, was guarded by monsters and surrounded by a moat filled with the tormented. Dante, protected by Virgil, entered the forbidden city, and viewed sights never before seen by living man.

(*Dante urges attack on the city of Florence, April 16, 1311.*)

Read from Dante's DIVINE COMEDY...................Vol. 20, pp. 32-39

17 **Benjamin Franklin—Book Salesman**

In 1731 there were not many books in America. Franklin saw the need for more books and by house-to-house canvassing persuaded Philadelphians to aid him in founding a public library which to-day stands as a lasting memorial to Franklin.

(*Benjamin Franklin died April 17, 1790.*)

Read from FRANKLIN'S AUTOBIOGRAPHY................Vol. 1, pp. 66-77

APRIL *Reading Guide*

18 **Ready for Adventures and Conquests**

Reading too many romances of knights and valorous deeds caused a poor Spanish gentleman to polish up his great-grandfather's armor, rechristen his old nag, and sally forth. "Don Quixote," besides holding a secure niche in literature as the work that quashed the romantic school of knight-errantry, is at the same time one of the most widely-read stories in the world.

(Cervantes receives the last sacraments April 18, 1616.)
Read from Cervantes' Don Quixote..................Vol. 14, pp. 17-28

19 **Battle of Concord**

(Fought April 19, 1775.)
Dr. Eliot says of the opening stanza of the "Concord Hymn": "In twenty-eight words here are the whole scene and all the essential circumstances . . . what an accurate, moving, immortal description is this!"

Read: Emerson's Concord Hymn.................Vol. 42, pp. 1245-1246

20 **Byron Gave His Life for Freedom**

England's romantic poet died while fighting against the Turks on the side of the Greeks. His poems, "The Isles of Greece" and "The Prisoner of Chillon," proclaim freedom.

(At Missolonghi, Greece, 37 guns honor Byron, April 20, 1824.)
Read: Byron's Poems............................Vol. 41, pp. 801-815

21 **Books as Windows to the Past**

Through the pages of a book the reader sees the life of past days. Carnivals, processions, battles, coronations, voyages—the whole history of the world and its people is revealed in a stupendous pageant. Taine was a Frenchman who wrote an unsurpassed history of English literature; its introduction reveals the unusual combination of an imaginative and an analytical style.

(H. A. Taine born April 21, 1828.)
Read from Introduction to English Literature....Vol. 39, pp. 410-418

22 **Happiness as a Duty**

Immanuel Kant, the most influential of German philosophers, taught that it was man's duty to be happy, for an unhappy man is tempted to sin. Seekers after happiness find aid and inspiration in Kant's writings.

(Immanuel Kant born April 22, 1724.)
Read from Fundamental Principles of Morals....Vol. 32, pp. 310-317

APRIL *Reading Guide*

23 **"If You Have Poison for Me, I Will Drink It"**
Shaken and disillusioned by the treachery of his elder daughter, King Lear suspected even the faithful Cordelia of evil designs. Her most tender efforts to comfort him failed to drive away the insistent specter of his madness.
(*Shakespeare died April 23, 1616.*)
Read from Shakespeare's KING LEAR...............Vol. 46, pp. 293-303

24 **Nineteen Million Elephants**
At the rate at which elephants naturally increase, Darwin estimated that in 750 years there could be nearly 19,000,000 elephants. But did Darwin consider the ravages of civilization and circuses?
Read from Darwin's ORIGIN OF SPECIES..............Vol. 11, pp. 74-86

25 **Mighty Rome Feared These Men**
Men who danced among sharp swords—who gambled with their lives—who took their women to the battlefields to encourage the brave and shame the cowardly—these were the primitive Germans who made Roman emperors tremble.
Read from Tacitus' ON GERMANY..................Vol. 33, pp. 106-120

26 **Do Miracles Still Happen**
Just what constitutes a miracle? Does Science indorse miracles? One wonders why such marvelous things do not happen often nowadays. Hume tells why.
(*David Hume born April 26, 1711.*)
Read from Hume ON MIRACLES...................Vol. 37, pp. 375-385

27 **He Dared to See Forbidden Beauty**
The Puritan world feared Beauty. Emerson, great American essayist and philosopher, declared that the world was made for beauty, and openly worshiped at beauty's shrine.
(*Emerson died April 27, 1882.*)
Read: Emerson's BEAUTY.........................Vol. 5, pp. 297-310

28 **"Vanity of Vanities," Saith the Preacher**
Three hundred years before Christ, a preacher in Jerusalem complained that there was no new thing under the sun. Everything considered new had really existed in the time of the fathers. Sophisticated and modern is this writer of 2,300 years ago.
Read from THE BOOK OF ECCLESIASTES.............Vol. 44, pp. 335-341

April *Reading Guide*

29 How I Got Rich—by Sindbad the Sailor

Sindbad, a poor man, recited woeful verses before the magnificent dwelling of Sindbad of the Sea. The great Sindbad, hearing him, invited the poor Sindbad to a feast and told the wonderful story of his fabulous fortune.

Read from The Thousand and One Nights..........Vol. 16, pp. 231-242

30 Washington's Dictum on Private Life

Washington declared that the strength of the new nation lay in the "pure and immutable principles of private morality." A free government, fortified by the virtues and affection of its citizens, can command the respect of the world.

(*Washington inaugurated April 30, 1789.*)

Read: Washington's First Inaugural Address........Vol. 43, pp. 225-228

"No testimony is sufficient to establish a miracle," wrote Hume, thus arousing bitter animosity in orthodox circles. Hume's searching treatment of miracles will stimulate to deeper thought upon this controversial subject. (See Reading Assignment for April 26th.)

THE SWEETEST PATH OF LIFE LEADS THROUGH THE AVENUES OF SCIENCE AND LEARNING.—Hume.

MAY

When the hounds of spring are on winter's traces,
The mother of months in meadow or plain
Fills the shadows and windy places
With lisp of leaves and ripple of rain. . .

SWINBURNE (Vol. 42, p. 1199)

1 What Would *You* Ask Judas Iscariot?

Once Hazlitt and his friends took to discussing the famous people they would like to meet—Guy Fawkes, Sir Isaac Newton,
Chaucer, Boccaccio, Cromwell, Garrick, and Judas.

Read: PERSONS ONE WOULD WISH TO HAVE SEEN......Vol. 27, pp. 270-283

2 First Sparks of Electricity

Everything has to have a beginning, so too with the science of
electricity. Here we learn the very rudiments, the inceptions
of science that have revolutionized the world. Faraday explains
in a simple way the truths of electricity.

Read: Faraday's MAGNETISM—ELECTRICITY...........Vol. 30, pp. 61-72

3 Why "Machiavellian"?

Traveling from court to court in the stirring days of the Renaissance, Machiavelli studied the intrigues of princes. His writings have affected the destiny of mighty dynasties.

(Machiavelli born May 3, 1469.)
Read from Machiavelli's THE PRINCE.................Vol. 36, pp. 7-17

4 A Champion of Science

When science was struggling for a place in popular education,
Huxley distinguished himself as its champion. While the arts
were to beautify life and increase pleasure, Huxley saw science
as a means of benefiting man's prosperity.

(Huxley born May 4, 1825.)
Read from SCIENCE AND CULTURE.................Vol. 28, pp. 209-219

5 Strange Adventures in Man's Clothes

Disguised as a man, a Russian noblewoman exploring the moun-
tains of Poland came upon a secret prison. Fate linked the
lives of this woman and the unknown prisoner.

(Calderon, after a life of adventure, died May 5, 1681.)
Read from Calderon's LIFE IS A DREAM...............Vol. 26, pp. 7-21

May *Reading Guide*

6 **A Poor Artist Defies a Rich Duke**

"Benvenuto, the figure cannot succeed in bronze," so spoke the patron Duke. Cellini, stung to fury, passionately burst out: "You do not understand art." Feverishly he began the casting of the statue—but read his own account of the tilt with the Duke.
Read from CELLINI'S AUTOBIOGRAPHY..............Vol. 31, pp. 373-384

7 **A Bishop Bargains**

A haughty aristocrat, who murdered his wife for enjoying life more than he, now bargaining for a new bride; a crafty bishop begging and bullying his heirs for a tomb richer than that of his rival; these are subjects of Browning's pen.
(*Robert Browning born May 7, 1812.*)
Read from BROWNING'S POEMS...................Vol. 42, pp. 1074-1078

8 **Behind the Screen in the School for Scandal**

Lady Teazle hides in haste when her husband is unexpectedly announced. Situations which set many tongues wagging and fed the fire of gossip in Scandal-land, startle the reader.
(*"School for Scandal" produced at Drury Lane, May 8, 1777.*)
Read from Sheridan's SCHOOL FOR SCANDAL..........Vol. 18, pp. 164-176

9 **Relation of Art to Freedom**

Who has ever thought the arts had anything to do with freedom? Schiller did. Forced by a German noble to enter a military school, he escaped. Struggling to achieve freedom, he wrote a series of letters on the relation of art to freedom.
(*Friedrich von Schiller died May 9, 1805.*)
Read: Schiller's ON ÆSTHETIC EDUCATION...........Vol. 32, pp. 209-217

10 **A Knight Among Cannibals**

Savages who drink the powdered bones of their dead mixed with wine, Amazons who hold riotous festivals, the worship of golden statues, all the primitive wonders of Guiana are described by the famous Elizabethan gallant, Sir Walter Raleigh.
Read from Raleigh's DISCOVERY OF GUIANA..........Vol. 33, pp. 326-341

11 **Latest Gossip in Malfi**

Latest news abroad in Malfi: The Duchess has run off with her butler. But this happened before the days of newspapers or radio, so Webster made from it an exciting play.
Read from Webster's THE DUCHESS OF MALFI........Vol. 47, pp. 721-737

May *Reading Guide*

12 **His Wife's Golden Hair Enshrined His Poems**

The manuscripts of many of the best poems of Rossetti were buried with his wife. Friends prevailed upon him to allow them to be exhumed—and these poems, once buried with the dead, are now a treasure of the living.

(*Rossetti born May 12, 1828.*)

Read: ROSSETTI'S POEMS...............Vol. 42, pp. 1149-1153, 1178-1181

13 **What Does Your Dog Think of You?**

Two dogs fell a-gossiping about their masters and about a dog's life among the humble Scotch folk. Each "rejoic'd they werena men but dogs; an' each took aff his several way."

Read: BURNS' THE TWA DOGS.......................Vol. 6, pp. 151-157

14 **Jenner's Amazing Smallpox Cure**

Edward Jenner found that disease in the heel of a horse, transmitted through a cow to the dairy attendants, was an agent in making human beings immune from smallpox. His amazing experiments inaugurated a new epoch.

(*Edward Jenner makes his first vaccination May 14, 1796.*)

Read: VACCINATION AGAINST SMALLPOX.............Vol. 38, pp. 145-154

15 **Glimpses Into the Beyond**

The best part of the Divine Comedy for a few minutes' reading is the "Inferno." There the reader finds the most vivid descriptions, the most startling and unforgettable pictures.

(*Dante born May 15, 1265.*)

Read from Dante's DIVINE COMEDY................Vol. 20, pp. 102-114

16 **Favorite Superstitions of Celtic Imagination**

Chessboards on which, of their own accord, black pieces played against white; chariots that swiftly turned hither and yon without a driver; pots in which a coward's meat would not cook— all these are woven into bewitching stories.

Read from THE POETRY OF THE CELTIC RACES.......Vol. 32, pp. 145-155

17 **An Honest Life's Reward**

Condemned for impiety, Socrates felt so justified in the virtue of his past action that instead of receiving a death sentence, he told the judges he should be maintained at public expense as a public benefactor.

Read: Plato's APOLOGY OF SOCRATES...................Vol. 2, pp. 24-30

May *Reading Guide*

18 The Night Life of Flowers

Flowers often tire of their stationary life and sometimes at night frolic away to a ball in a beautiful castle. Thus a fanciful story-teller accounts for their drooping condition in the morning.

Read: ANDERSEN'S TALES.........................Vol. 17, pp. 334-341

19 Golden Advice on Manners

When a man is invited to a banquet he must be satisfied with the dishes put before him. Epictetus reasoned that man should be content with what life offers, and in serenity find happiness.

Read: Epictetus' GOLDEN SAYINGS....................Vol. 2, pp. 128-138

20 Shakespeare's Finest Work

The most concentrated beauty of Shakespeare's unbounded creative genius is found in his sonnets. Written as personal messages to friends and not intended for publication, they reveal the inner Shakespeare more truly than do any of his great plays.

(Sonnets entered in the London Stationers' Register, May 20. 1609.)

Read from Shakespeare's SONNETS..................Vol. 40, pp. 270-276

21 An Honest Man Defined

The sharp tongue of Alexander Pope made him celebrated, yet widely feared. In a representative product of his versatile pen, he gracefully combines his flashing wit with sage advice.

(Alexander Pope born May 21, 1688.)

Read from Pope's ESSAY ON MAN................ ....Vol. 40, pp. 430-440

22 True Love in Difficulty

Because of a fancy for a peasant girl, the tyrannical lord of an Italian village sent desperadoes to threaten the priest if he married the girl to her village lover.

(Manzoni died May 22, 1873.)

Read from Manzoni's I PROMESSI SPOSI.................Vol. 21, pp. 7-24

23 A Plea for an Unfortunate

From the river her body was tenderly lifted—the girl who could find no place in the vast city. Thomas Hood pleads for her—eloquently and justly. Read this gem of pathos.

(Thomas Hood born May 23, 1799.)

Read: HOOD'S POEMS............................Vol. 41, pp. 907-911

May *Reading Guide*

24   They Had No Money—Yet Bought and Sold

Debts were not always paid in money. Not so long ago the butcher paid for his keg of beer with a slab of beef, and oxen were exchanged for land and wives. Adam Smith tells the interesting story of the origin and use of money.

Read from Adam Smith's WEALTH OF NATIONS . . . . Vol. 10, pp. 27-33

25   Do What You Fear

Emerson startled the world by fearlessly declaring his beliefs. Such apparent paradoxes as we find in his inspirational essay, "Heroism," makes him the most stimulating yet profound thinker America has produced.

(Emerson born May 25, 1803.)

Read: Emerson's HEROISM . . . . Vol. 5, pp. 121-131

26   Daughter Declares Her Love

Goneril and Regan falsely swore they loved their father, King Lear, more than life itself. Cordelia could find no words to express her sincere devotion. Then King Lear made the decision that started a series of exciting events.

(Shakespeare's first daughter, Susanna, baptized May 26, 1583.)

Read from Shakespeare's KING LEAR . . . . Vol. 46, pp. 215-225

27   Lessing's Courageous Stand for Toleration

To advance freedom of thought, Lessing published an essay of one hundred paragraphs outlining the history of religion. The wrath of orthodox churchmen was hurled at his head, and Lessing was left alone to defend his daring theories.

Read from THE EDUCATION OF THE HUMAN RACE . . . . . . Vol. 32, pp. 185-195

28   Master of Melodious Lyrics

Any one of these poems, "The Harp That Once Through Tara's Halls," "The Last Rose of Summer," "The Light of Other Days," would alone have made Moore immortal.

(Thomas Moore born May 28, 1779.)

Read: MOORE'S POEMS . . . . Vol. 41, pp. 816-822

29   Adventures in Bagdad

A Bagdad merchant dreamed of the money he would make from the sale of a tray of glassware, and of marrying the king's daughter. But, daydreaming, he kicked over the tray.

Read from THE THOUSAND AND ONE NIGHTS . . . . Vol. 16, pp. 177-184

MAY *Reading Guide*

30 **When the Throb of the War Drum Is Stifl'd**
(*Memorial Day.*)
At the close of the war, a torn and bleeding nation set about to rebuild its shattered frame. The result was a stronger nation rising from an almost disrupted union.
Read: Longfellow's THE BUILDING OF THE SHIP....Vol. 42, pp. 1280-1290

31 **America's Most Surprising Poet**
Walt Whitman is the most original and startling of modern poets. An irony of his life is that while he wrote for the contemporary masses, only a limited number of followers appreciated his genius, now universally recognized.
(*Walt Whitman born May 31, 1819.*)
Read: Whitman's PREFACE TO LEAVES OF GRASS.......Vol. 39, pp. 388-398

Edward Jenner laid the foundation for the making of modern small-pox vaccine. He made his first experiment in 1796 by inoculating a boy of eight. (See Reading Assignment for May 14th.)

THE GENERAL PRINCIPLES OF ANY STUDY YOU MAY LEARN BY BOOKS AT HOME.—NEWMAN.

JUNE

When shepherds pipe on oaten straws,
And merry larks are ploughmen's clocks,
When turtles tread, and rooks, and daws,
And maidens bleach their summer smocks.

SHAKESPEARE (Vol. 40, p. 265)

1 Thrilling Play by Tutor of Shakespeare

For the best blank verse in English, read "Dr. Faustus," the masterpiece of Marlowe, who gave Shakespeare lessons in playwriting. This genius knew the secret of gripping drama.
(Marlowe died June 1, 1593.)
Read from Marlowe's DR. FAUSTUS................Vol. 19, pp. 241-250

2 "Back to Nature" in the Seventeenth Century

A "Back to Nature" movement in the seventeenth century was headed by Rousseau, who believed that civilization was degrading. To save money for his work, he entrusted each of his children to the tender mercies of a foundling house.
(Jean Jacques Rousseau born June 2, 1712.)
Read from Rousseau's A SAVOYARD VICAR..........Vol. 34, pp. 239-249

3 Pulse Aids Epochal Discoveries

Galileo, by holding his pulse while watching a swinging cathedral lamp, evolved a theory that made clocks possible. Harvey, by feeling his pulse, educed that arteries carry blood.
(Dr. William Harvey died June 3, 1657.)
Read from MOTION OF THE HEART AND BLOOD..........Vol. 38, pp. 75-86

4 'Neath the Iron Hand of Spain

Spain sent the Duke of Alva to subdue the Netherlands. In quelling disorder he killed the people's hero, Count Egmont. From this story Goethe made a famous play.
(Egmont sentenced to death June 4, 1658.)
Read from Goethe's EGMONT.....................Vol. 19, pp. 253-259

5 The Rent of Land from Human Food

Even to-day rent is paid in terms of human food. It sounds primitive, but it happens right at your door—here in the United States, in compliance with a law as old as man.
(Adam Smith born June 5, 1723.)
Read from Adam Smith's WEALTH OF NATIONS.......Vol. 10, pp. 149-157

June *Reading Guide*

6 A Shrill Cry in the Night!

A crew faced the hazardous prospect of rounding the bleak Cape Horn in midwinter. Imagine the terror when a sudden scream pierced the misery-laden air. What was it? A man overboard or a lost soul?

(R. H. Dana on watch, night of June 6, 1836.)
Read from Dana's TWO YEARS BEFORE THE MAST......Vol. 23, pp. 285-295

7 "There's Rosemary—that's for Remembrance!"

Do you know the rest of Ophelia's famous line? "Hamlet" is the most popular play in the entire world. It has been quoted so often that reading it is like meeting an old friend.

(Edwin Booth, famed Shakespearian actor, died June 7, 1893.)
Read from HAMLET..............................Vol. 46, pp. 176-183

8 Eloquence Wins Over Prejudice

The plain, homely appearance of Woolman impressed unfavorably the orthodox Quakers in London whom he was sent to meet. They told him his coming was not necessary. But Woolman spoke with such simplicity and sincerity that even those most opposed became his friends.

(John Woolman arrives in London for Friends' meeting, June 8, 1772.)
Read from WOOLMAN'S JOURNAL....................Vol. 1, pp. 302-312

9 Enchanting Songs of David

The songs of David pleased King Saul, but when David became too popular with the people, the king feared for his throne and banished him.

Read from THE PSALMS.........................Vol. 44, pp. 168-179

10 Horrible Prophecy Fulfilled

King Œdipus of Thebes as a babe was abandoned on Mount Cithæron to die. Years after he was thought dead he returns to Thebes and unknowingly slays his father, marries his mother—and thus fulfills the word of the oracle.

Read from Sophocles' ŒDIPUS, KING OF THEBES........Vol. 8, pp. 209-223

11 He Sang of His Beautiful Elizabeth

To commemorate his marriage to the beautiful Elizabeth, Spenser wrote one of the most enchanting nuptial hymns.

(Edmund Spenser married Elizabeth Boyle, June 11, 1594.)
Read: Spenser's THE EPITHALAMIUM..............Vol. 40, pp. 234-245

JUNE *Reading Guide*

12 Vishnu Holds Up a Battle
Two armies of ancient India were about to engage in a momentous battle. Arjuna, heroic leader of the Pandu hosts, foreseeing great slaughter, hesitates. He implores the divine Vishnu to intervene. The conversation of the warrior and the god is a gem of Hindu literature.
Read from THE BHAGAVAD-GITA.....................Vol. 45, pp. 785-798

13 Athens Flouts Aristides
Athenians gave Aristides the title of "The Just." Later they wanted to banish him. One voter wanted Aristides banished merely because he was weary of hearing him called "The Just."
Read from Plutarch's ARISTIDES......................Vol. 12, pp. 85-94

14 A Philosopher Prefers Prison Cell
Socrates unceasingly strove for beauty, truth, and perfection. Sentenced to death on a false charge, he refused to escape from the death cell, even when opportunity was offered.
Read: Plato's CRITO...............................Vol. 2, pp. 31-43

15 Strikers Storm the Tower of London
Led by Wat Tyler in 1381, great troops of villagers and rustics marched on London—laid siege to the Tower—sacked the apartments of the King and murdered his ministers. Froissart gives first-hand information of this rebellion.
(*Wat Tyler's Rebellion suppressed June 15, 1381.*)
Read from Froissart's WAT TYLER'S REBELLION.........Vol. 35, pp. 60-72

16 Spirits at the Top of the World
The inaccessible mountain tops were ever venerated as the haunts of all mysteries. Manfred, hero of Byron's play, seeks upon the high Alps the aid of spirits, specters, and goblins. What unearthly adventures await him!
(*Byron publishes "Manfred," June 16, 1817.*)
Read from Byron's MANFRED......................Vol. 18, pp. 415-428

17 Risked His Scalp in Prayer
John Eliot put his life at the mercy of the redmen to get them to listen to his preachings. He wrote vividly about his settlements of Christian Indians. Now villages and Indians have disappeared. Only his story remains.
(*John Eliot holds Indian prayer meeting June 17, 1670.*)
Read: Eliot's BRIEF NARRATIVE....................Vol. 43, pp. 138-146

JUNE *Reading Guide*

18 Cinderella Lives To-day

Cinderella inspires all alike—the artist's brush, the author's pen, the child's fancy. To-day she is a living, vital character to be seen on stage and screen. No one ever forgets her lightning change.
Read from GRIMM'S TALES........................Vol. 17, pp. 98-104

19 Freaks of the Dog Fad in England

A writer of Elizabethan times said that no other country had as many dogs as England. Once Henry VII ordered all mastiffs to be hung because they "durst presume to fight against the lion," England's regal beast.
Read: Holinshed's OUR ENGLISH DOGS..............Vol. 35, pp. 350-356

20 No Salt for These Birds

Galapagos Islands are the home of fearless birds, to which horses, cows, and men are only roosting places. Darwin saw the South Pacific when few travelers knew that wonderland.
Read from Darwin's VOYAGE OF THE BEAGLE........Vol. 29, pp. 403-413

21 Would You Converse with Royalty?

Why gossip with lesser persons when you might be talking to queens and kings? Just how we may get to talk to queens and kings, Ruskin delightfully points out and escorts us to the very doors of the audience chamber.
Read from Ruskin's SESAME........................Vol. 28, pp. 99-110

22 Pliny Tells Ghost Stories

Pliny, who lived in the first century after Christ, tells of a ghost who dragged his jangling chains through a house in Athens and so terrified the inmates that they fled panic-stricken. But the ghost met his equal.
Read from Pliny's LETTERS........................Vol. 9, pp. 311-314

23 Greek Scholar at Three

John Stuart Mill—one of the greatest intellects in England—tells how his father educated him. At the early age of three years he began the study of Greek, and at twelve started writing a book of his own.
(James Mill, father of John Stuart Mill, died June 23, 1836.)
Read from Mill's AUTOBIOGRAPHY......................Vol. 25, pp. 9-20

JUNE *Reading Guide*

24   Had No Right Hand

A handsome young man was seen to eat only with his left hand, which was contrary to the customs of Arabia. The youth, when urged, told why he used only his left hand, and revealed a story of love and adventure and the lover's need for gold—all happening in ancient Cairo.

Read from THE THOUSAND AND ONE NIGHTS.........Vol. 16, pp. 120-133

25   Advice to Virgins from a Wise Man

"Gather ye rosebuds while ye may, Old Time is still a-flying; And this same flower that smiles today, to-morrow will be dying?" Herrick was only a humble country minister with a wealth of wisdom and a keen appreciation of life, which he expressed in lyrics of wonderful beauty and melody.

Read: HERRICK's POEMS...........................Vol. 40, pp. 334-340

26   In the Lair of the Green-Eyed Monster

At the bottom of the ocean was the home of the monster who had desolated the king's halls. Beowulf, bravest of warriors, descended beneath the waves to fight the beast. The king's men, waiting above, saw the waves become colored with blood. Hero or monster—who had won?

Read from BEOWULF..............................Vol. 49, pp. 45-50

27   Do You Take Poison Daily?

There is a human trait most poisonous to a man's blood. Man seeks to avoid it because he knows that it lies like a curse upon him. Just what is the poisonous human failing? Who are most subject to it? Bacon tells you in one of his best essays.

(*Francis Bacon enrolled at Cambridge University, June 27, 1576.*)
Read from BACON's ESSAYS..........................Vol. 3, pp. 22-26

28   Pages from the Pampas Book of Etiquette

A very definite etiquette is followed by a stranger on the vast plains of South America. "Ave Maria" is the common saluta-tion. If the stranger is on horseback, he does not alight until invited to do so by his host. Once in the house, the stranger must converse a while before asking shelter for the night.

Read from Darwin's VOYAGE OF THE BEAGLE...........Vol. 29, pp. 51-60

JUNE *Reading Guide*

29 "Is That a Dagger I See Before Me?"

Macbeth, spurred on by the ambitious and crafty Lady Macbeth, committed murder to secure the crown of Scotland. But he paid dearly for his gain. Ghostly guests appeared at his banquet and threatened him with dire threats.

(*Shakespeare's Globe Theatre burned June 29, 1613.*)

Read from Shakespeare's MACBETH................Vol. 46, pp. 357-365

30 Rather King Than Majority

"Democracy" has not always been the choice of oppressed people. The tyranny of the majority is a recognized evil as harmful as the misrule of a king. And rather than exchange a lesser evil for a greater, a rule by king has often been preferred to a republic.

Read: Mill's ON LIBERTY........................Vol. 25, pp. 195-203

Escape from prison is offered Socrates, but his conscientious principles regarding man's relations to the laws caused him to refuse this opportunity and face the death decreed by his judges. (See Reading Assignment for June 14.)

IF YOU READ TEN PAGES OF A GOOD BOOK, LETTER BY LETTER—THAT IS TO SAY, WITH REAL ACCURACY—YOU ARE FOREVERMORE IN SOME MEASURE AN EDUCATED PERSON.—JOHN RUSKIN.

JULY

Rosy summer next advancing, . . .
On Calpe's olive-shaded steep
Or India's citron-cover'd isles. . . .

CAMPBELL (Vol. 41, p. 772)

1 Darwin Not First Evolutionist
While Darwin was working on his theory of evolution, another scientist independently arrived at the same conclusions. Darwin, then, was not the first to study evolution.
(*Darwin publishes outline of "Origin of Species," July 1, 1858.*)
Read from Darwin's ORIGIN OF SPECIES.............Vol. 11, pp. 5-17

2 "Julius" Becomes "July"
So that the date for certain festivals would not fall one year in midwinter and in the heat of summer another year, Cæsar reformed the calendar. July was named for him.
Read from Plutarch's CÆSAR.....................Vol. 12, pp. 310-315

3 Gettysburg by an Eyewitness
An officer in that momentous battle narrates every major action of both armies. Thus we see the swarming lines of Confederates advance—the hand-to-hand struggle.
(*Battle of Gettysburg, July 1-3, 1863.*)
Read from Haskell's BATTLE OF GETTYSBURG........Vol. 43, pp. 326-335

4 Some Chose to Remain British Subjects
(*Independence Day.*)
Some Americans preferred to be loyal to England and did not want independent government. Their hesitation is better understood when the finality of the Declaration is realized.
Read: DECLARATION OF INDEPENDENCE.............Vol. 43, pp. 150-155

5 A Tailor Entertains a King
Here is another of those fanciful Oriental stories that proclaims the democracy of Eastern despotism. A tailor might talk with a king and receive either a death sentence or the office of Grand Vizier as a reward.
Read from THE THOUSAND AND ONE NIGHTS.........Vol. 16, pp. 149-162

July *Reading Guide*

6 The Origin of "Utopia"

When Europe was suffering from evil rulers, heavy taxes, and despair, Sir Thomas More dreamed of a happy land where an intelligently managed state perfected happiness.

(*Sir Thomas More executed, July 6, 1535.*)
Read from More's UTOPIA.........................Vol. 36, pp. 135-142

7 Scandal That Lurked Behind Lace and Powder

The painted lips of the eighteenth century ladies and gallants vied with one another in whispering scathing gossip, in gleefully furthering the destruction of a good name. Sheridan depicts this gay world with a brilliant spicy pen.

(*Sheridan buried in Westminster Abbey, July 7, 1816.*)
Read from Sheridan's SCHOOL FOR SCANDAL.........Vol. 18, pp. 115-128

8 Italy's Fair Assassin

When the monstrous Cenci forced his daughter Beatrice into a horrible situation, she revolted and boldly struck for freedom. Shelley tells her pitiful story in one of his best works.

(*Percy Bysshe Shelley drowned, July 8, 1822.*)
Read from Shelley's CENCI.......................Vol. 18, pp. 288-300

9 A Little Lying Now and Then

"What is Truth?" asked Pilate. For an answer Bacon discourses not on human nature as it should be, but as it is. These shrewd observations on making a life and a living admit occasional departures from truth.

(*Bacon becomes Privy Councilor, July 9, 1616.*)
Read from BACON'S ESSAYS...........................Vol. 3, pp. 7-19

10 America's First Immigrants

The shadow of a phantom cast upon the cradle of Snorri, the first white child born in America, was a warning of an Indian attack on the settlement of courageous Norsemen who had risked the terrors of unknown seas to visit "Wineland."

Read from THE VOYAGES TO VINLAND................Vol. 43. pp. 14-20

11 Star Gazing—A Cure for Tired Minds

The greatest spectacle offered man is a view of the magnificent vault of heaven. Under the stupendous arch of the Milky Way the cares of the world roll off.

(*Newcomb died July 11, 1909.*)
Read: Newcomb's THE EXTENT OF THE UNIVERSE......Vol. 30, pp. 311-321

JULY *Reading Guide*

12 But He Walked!

Thoreau's individuality was unique and original. He had no
profession; he never married; he never went to church; he never
voted or paid taxes; he never smoked; he never drank wine. His
amusement was walking, to observe and meditate.
(Henry David Thoreau born July 12, 1817.)
Read from Thoreau's WALKING.....................Vol. 28, pp. 395-405

13 Athenians Also Complained of Taxes

Pericles used public money to beautify Athens. The citizens
protested against the expense, as citizens in all ages do. By a
clever stroke Pericles won their support to his ambitious plans.
Read from Plutarch's PERICLES.......................Vol. 12, pp. 47-57

14 The French People Triumph

(The Bastille surrendered, July 14, 1789.)
What the Fourth of July is to Americans, the Fourteenth of July
is to Frenchmen. It commemorates an oppressive tyranny over-
thrown by a freedom-loving people.
Read from Burke's THE REVOLUTION IN FRANCE......Vol. 24, pp. 268-273

15 When Elizabeth Dined

Meals in the houses of the gentry and noblemen in Elizabethan
England were taken most seriously. No one spoke. Holinshed
records the strange table etiquette of our ancestors.
(Queen Elizabeth entertained at Kenilworth, July 15, 1575.)
Read from HOLINSHED's CHRONICLES...............Vol. 35, pp. 271-288

16 The Mohammedan Jesus

The sacred book of the Moslems, the Koran, gives an account of
the birth of Christ. The Koran gives Jesus a high position among
the prophets but holds the first place for Mohammed.
(Beginning of Moslem era of time, July 16, 622 A. D.)
Read from THE KORAN..........................Vol. 45, pp. 908-913

17 A Throne for Son or Stepson?

Phædre first persecuted Hippolytus, her handsome stepson, then
loved him. Suddenly he and her own son became rivals for the
throne. Should she push her son's claims or let Hippolytus take
the crown?
(Racine elected to French Academy, July 17, 1673.)
Read from Racine's PHÆDRE.......................Vol. 26, pp. 133-148

July *Reading Guide*

18 They Loved in Vain

"Browning's play has thrown me into a perfect passion of sorrow," wrote Charles Dickens of "The Blot in the 'Scutcheon." Like Shakespeare's Juliet, Browning's Mildred plays the rôle of a youthful lover in a tragic drama.

Read from Browning's BLOT IN THE 'SCUTCHEON......Vol. 18, pp. 359-368

19 She Wanted Heroes All to Herself

The famous gallant who spread his gorgeous cloak so the dainty slipper of his queen would be unspotted, soon lost the high favor this action won for him. In spite of his glorious voyages, Raleigh condemned himself when he fell in love with another woman.

(Sir Walter Raleigh imprisoned July 19, 1603.)
Read from Raleigh's DISCOVERY OF GUIANA..........Vol. 33, pp. 311-320

20 A Cobbler in Jail

John Bunyan, imprisoned for preaching without a license, gave to the world "Pilgrim's Progress," the greatest allegory in any language, second only to the Bible.

Read from Bunyan's PILGRIM'S PROGRESS.............Vol. 15, pp. 59-69

21 Scotland's Own Poet

The songs of Burns are the links, the watchwords, the symbols of the Scots. He is the last of the ballad singers. In his works are preserved the best songs of his people.

(Robert Burns died July 21, 1796.)
Read from BURNS' POEMS.............................Vol. 6, pp. 70-79

22 Trapped in a Cave with a Frenzied Giant

Odysseus was wrecked with his men on an island inhabited by one-eyed giants. Trapped in the cave of a giant who gobbled up some of the crew for supper, the cunning Odysseus blinded the giant and rescued the survivors of his crew.

Read from Homer's ODYSSEY.....................Vol. 22, pp. 120-129

23 Friendship Above Love?

There are styles in friendship as well as in clothes. The mode of friendship of Bacon's time went out with plumed hats and long hose. But Bacon knew the true test of a friend.

(Francis Bacon knighted, July 23, 1603.)
Read from BACON'S ESSAYS............................Vol. 3, pp. 65-72

July *Reading Guide*

24 Indian Sorcery Blamed for an Earthquake

Darwin visited a South American city ruined by an earthquake. There he heard the superstitious account of the phenomenon. The ignorant people accused Indian women of bewitching the volcano. But Darwin has another explanation.

Read from Darwin's THE VOYAGE OF THE BEAGLE...... Vol. 29, pp. 306-316

25 A Goddess and Her Mortal Lover

Brynhild, Woden's daughter, carried the dead heroes to Valhalla where they could feast and fight without dying; until a sin divested her of divinity, and she fell in love with Sigurd.

Read: LAY OF BRYNHILD.......................... Vol. 49, pp. 391-395

26 Peace Amid Strife

While Europe was shaken with wars, Thomas à Kempis lived in happy seclusion in his convent. His writings convincingly reflect the serenity and happiness of a man who has found peace— a peace that surpasses all understanding.

(*Thomas à Kempis died July 26, 1471.*)
Read from Thomas à Kempis...................... Vol. 7, pp. 205-211

27 Once Surgeons Operated in Frock Coats

The use of antiseptics in surgery is new. Hardly more than a half century ago surgeons operated in frock coats. Lord Lister, surgeon to Queen Victoria, was among the first to advocate scrupulous cleanliness in dressing wounds.

(*Lister publishes paper on antiseptic treatment, July 27, 1867.*)
Read: ON THE ANTISEPTIC PRINCIPLES............. Vol. 38, pp. 257-267

28 An Idyl of Agriculture

Cowley portrays the ideal life—that of a farmer, and blazons it forth in heraldry. "A plow in a field arable"—to him, the most honorable of all emblems.

(*Abraham Cowley died July 28, 1667.*)
Read: Cowley's OF AGRICULTURE.................... Vol. 27, pp. 61-69

29 Stonehenge—England's Unsolved Mystery

Stonehenge, that group of huge, rudely architectural stones on a vast plain in England, was erected no man knows when, nor why, nor how. Emerson, America's greatest thinker, visited this monument and was amazed at the "uncanny stones."

Read: Emerson's STONEHENGE...................... Vol. 5, pp. 453-462

July *Reading Guide*

30 **The First English Colony in North America**

When the whole coast of America north of Florida was free to the first comer, Sir Humphrey Gilbert naïvely chose to settle on the rugged shores of Newfoundland. Read the glowing account of his great adventure "to plant Christian inhabitants in places convenient."

(Gilbert lands at Newfoundland near St. John's, July 30, 1583.)

Read: Gilbert's Voyage to Newfoundland..........Vol. 33, pp. 263-273

31 **Charm School for Women**

Lack of education, writes Defoe, makes a woman "turbulent, clamorous, noisy—" Defoe defied his generation and preached equal education for women. To-day we have co-education, but have we the benefits Defoe predicted?

(Defoe pilloried for defiance of public opinion, July 31, 1703.)

Read: Defoe's Education of Women...............Vol. 27, pp. 148-150

"Between the Devil and the Deep Sea" was originated by Homer, who wrote it "Between Scylla and Charybdis." Sailing through this narrow channel was one of the many exciting adventures of Odysseus. (See Reading Assignment for July 22d.)

THE TRUE UNIVERSITY OF OUR DAYS IS A COLLECTION OF BOOKS.—Carlyle.

AUGUST

Now westlin winds and slaught'ring guns
Bring Autumn's pleasant weather. . . .
Now waving grain, wide o'er the plain,
Delights the weary farmer. . . .

BURNS (Vol. 6, p. 45)

1 His Influence Still Lives

Steadfast allegiance to duty, simple living and adherence to plain, honest, homely doctrines are Calvin's principles. Are not these same old-fashioned truths followed to-day?

(Calvin issues "Dedication," Aug. 1, 1536.)
Read from Calvin's DEDICATION......................Vol. 39, pp. 27-33

2 Poems from a Heart of Love

"Here is the pleasant place—and nothing wanting is, save She, alas!" How often we too are faced with like adversity. So sings Drummond—a master songster and composer.

Read from DRUMMOND'S POEMS...................Vol. 40, pp. 326-330

3 When the Greeks Sacked Troy

They battered down the palace gates and ravaged with fire and sword the chambers of King Priam's hundred wives. Through halls resounding with shrieks of terror, Priam and his household fled to sanctuary.

Read from Virgil's ÆNEID........................Vol. 13, pp. 110-117

4 World's Greatest Bedtime Stories

Hans Christian Andersen had an extraordinary capacity for amusing children. Were he living to-day he might be in great demand as a radio bedtime story man.

(H. C. Andersen died Aug. 4, 1875.)
Read: ANDERSEN'S TALES........................Vol. 17, pp. 221-230

5 Joys of the Simple Life

"Cotter's Saturday Night" for generations to come will remain the choicest picture of Scotch home life. Into this poem Burns instills the sense of all-pervading peace and happiness that comes at the end of a well-spent day.

(Robert Burns married Jean Armour, Aug. 5, 1788.)
Read: Burns' COTTERS' SATURDAY NIGHT..............Vol. 6, pp. 134-140

August *Reading Guide*

6 A Prophet of Aerial Warfare

"For I dipt into the future—saw the nation's airy navies grappling in the central blue." We are amazed at the accuracy of Tennyson's prediction. But he also foretells "the federation of the world"—yet to be fulfilled.

(Alfred Lord Tennyson born Aug. 6, 1809.)

Read: Tennyson's LOCKSLEY HALL.................Vol. 42, pp. 979-986

7 The Last Golden Words of Socrates

The death sentence of Socrates could not be executed until the return of the sacred ship from Delos. One day his friends learned that the ship had returned. They hastened to the prison to listen to the last words of Athens' sage.

Read from Plato's PHÆDO...........................Vol. 2, pp. 45-54

8 Men Transformed by Circe's Wand

Unfavorable winds sent by angry gods blew the ships of Odysseus far off their course. The sailors were cast upon a remote island, governed by an enchantress where, for their coarse manners, they were put under a magic spell.

Read from Homer's ODYSSEY......................Vol. 22, pp. 133-144

9 English Bridal Party Jailed

Minister and witness, bride and groom were arrested by an enraged father when John Donne married his employer's niece. Donne was soon released, but he found himself without money, position or bride.

(Isaak Walton born Aug. 9, 1593.)

Read from Walton's LIFE OF DR. DONNE...........Vol. 15, pp. 326-334

10 "Give Them Cake," said the Queen

When the people of Paris howled because they had no bread to eat, Queen Marie Antoinette exclaimed: "Well, then, let them eat cake!" Such an attitude hastened the revolution.

(French royal family imprisoned, Aug. 10, 1792.)

Read from Burke's THE REVOLUTION IN FRANCE......Vol. 24, pp. 143-157

11 Clever Repartee of Epictetus

Epictetus advises that if a person speaks ill of you, make no defense, but answer: "He surely knew not of my other faults, else he would not have mentioned these only."

Read from Epictetus' GOLDEN SAYINGS................Vol. 2, pp. 176-182

August *Reading Guide*

12 Zekle's Courtin'

Huldy, the rustic belle, sat alone peeling apples. She was bashful in her consciousness that Zekle would come soon. When he did, she merely blushed and timidly said: "Ma's sprinklin' clo'es," and then—

Read: LOWELL'S POEMS.........................Vol. 42, pp. 1376-1379

13 Too Close to See the Battle

(Battle of Blenheim, Aug. 13, 1704.)

England and France came to battle near Blenheim. Years later the people of Blenheim called it a "famous victory," but could not tell whose victory it was.

Read: Southey's AFTER BLENHEIM and other poems....Vol. 41, pp. 732-735

14 A College Boy Goes to Sea

Leaving Harvard on account of ill health, Dana sought adventure and thrilling experience aboard a sailing vessel that rounded Cape Horn. He turned the dangers, hardships, and keen joys of a sailor's life into a fascinating story.

(Dana begins famous two-year voyage, Aug. 14, 1834.)

Read from Dana's TWO YEARS BEFORE THE MAST.......Vol. 23, pp. 30-37

15 Into Death's Face He Flung This Song

(Roland died at Roncesvaux, Aug. 15, 778.)

Charlemagne's rear guard was attacked by the Basques in the valley of Roncesvaux. Roland, its leader, fought a courageous fight, and, though conquered, became immortal.

Read from THE SONG OF ROLAND..................Vol. 49, pp. 166-173

16 Inspiring Ritual of Temple Worship

David—the psalm singer—knew the wondrous ways of the Lord and praised Him in his psalms. Burdened souls in all ages have found comfort in these songs that once were used in the gorgeous ritual of Jerusalem's temple.

Read from THE PSALMS...........................Vol. 44, pp. 286-295

17 Three Walls Luther Saw

Luther declared that the unreformed church had drawn its doctrines like three walls so closely about the people that they served not as protection but were the cause of untold misery and distress. This he hoped to relieve by the Reformation.

Read: Luther's ADDRESS TO THE NOBILITY...........Vol. 36, pp. 263-275

August *Reading Guide*

18 **"I Took Her by the Hair and Dragged Her Up and Down"**
In Cellini's day the model's life was a hazardous one. Cellini's Autobiography reveals how some models were treated. You will find it more thrilling than the most modern novel.
Read from CELLINI'S AUTOBIOGRAPHY . . . . Vol. 31, pp. 312-323

19 **Roses Boiled in Wine**
Astonishing treatments and cures are related by Ambroise Paré, famed surgeon of the fifteenth century. One remedy, for instance, used to cure a distinguished nobleman, was red roses boiled in white wine,—and it was effective.
Read from Paré's JOURNEYS IN DIVERSE PLACES . . . . Vol. 38, pp. 50-58

20 **Plot Against Eve**
Driven from Heaven, Satan meditated revenge. He decided his greatest opportunity to injure God was to bring sin to mankind. Satan's plot against Eve is told by Milton.
("Paradise Lost" published Aug. 20, 1667.)
Read from Milton's PARADISE LOST . . . . Vol. 4, pp. 154-164

21 **Hidden Treasures in an Old Book**
A certain man was willed a Bible. He scorned the legacy until one day, penniless and downcast, he turned to the book for consolation. Imagine his amazement on finding hundred dollar bills between the pages. St. Augustine explains how he found even greater treasures in the Bible.
Read from CONFESSIONS OF ST. AUGUSTINE . . . . Vol. 7, pp. 118-126

22 **Aboard the Old Sailing Ships**
In the days when sailing ships plied the seven seas, common sailors were often subject to a brutal captain whose whim was law. Dana, a Boston college boy, makes an exciting story of his sea experiences.
Read from Dana's TWO YEARS BEFORE THE MAST . . . . . . Vol. 23, pp. 99-111

23 **Which Is a Beautiful Woman?**
The Hottentot thinks his wife beautiful. Every American believes his wife also to be beautiful. But the American and the Hottentot are quite different. What, after all, is Beauty?
Read from Burke's ON THE SUBLIME AND BEAUTIFUL . . . . Vol. 24, pp. 78-88

August *Reading Guide*

24 Survivor's Story of Vesuvius
(Pliny witnessed eruption of Vesuvius, Aug. 24, 79 A. D.)
The eruption of Vesuvius that demolished Pompeii and buried thousands of people was witnessed by Pliny. He describes his panic-stricken flight with his mother from the doomed villa through falling ashes and sulphurous fumes. His famous uncle, the elder Pliny, lost his life while investigating the eruption and aiding refugees.
Read from Pliny's LETTERS......................Vol. 9, pp. 284-291

25 Britain Saved by a Full Moon
We to-day know that there is a direct relation between the moon and tides. When Julius Cæsar went to conquer Britain his transports were wrecked because he did not know the tides on the English coast; a knowledge of which might have changed the whole course of history.
(Kelvin delivers lecture on "Tides," Aug. 25, 1882.)
Read from Kelvin's TIDES......................Vol. 30, pp. 274-285

26 The Prince of Wales Wins His Spurs
(Battle of Crecy, Aug. 26, 1346.)
A brilliant victory for the English king was gained in this battle, a fight in which vast numbers of French nobility, many princes, and the aged King John of Bohemia were slain. Froissart describes all in detail.
Read from FROISSART'S CHRONICLES..................Vol. 35, pp. 27-33

27 Priceless Treasures of Memory
"A man's a man for a' that." "Should auld acquaintance be forgot." "To see her is to love her and love but her forever." "Flow gently, sweet Afton." Every stanza of Burns is treasured. How many have you stored up?
Read from Burns' POEMS AND SONGS........Vol. 6, pp. 317, 417, 442, 511

28 The World's Love Tragedy
"Almighty God, I am undone." With this cry of despair, Margaret witnessed the fiendish work of Faust, her lover, who bartered his immortal soul for worldly pleasure. A thrilling drama, based on a famous medieval legend.
(Johann Wolfgang Goethe born Aug. 28, 1749.)
Read from Goethe's FAUST......................Vol. 19, pp. 158-167

AUGUST *Reading Guide*

29 Cleopatra Bewitches Mark Antony

Cleopatra rode to meet Antony in a gilded barge with sails of purple; oars of silver beat time to the music of flutes and fifes and harps. She went as Venus, and her attendants were dressed as Cupids and Nymphs.

(Cleopatra dies after Antony's suicide, Aug. 29, 30 B. C.)

Read from Plutarch's ANTONY......................Vol. 12, pp. 339-349

30 Simple Life in a Palace

Every luxury, all the wealth in the world at his command—yet Marcus Aurelius, Emperor of haughty Rome, led a simple life even in a palace. He left his secret in his "Meditations."

Read from Marcus Aurelius' MEDITATIONS...........Vol. 2, pp. 222-228

31 America's Greatest Thinker

Emerson was included in Dr. Eliot's recent selection of the world's ten greatest educators of all time. Here the great thinker discusses this force within man that makes him a scholar.

(Emerson delivers "American Scholar" lecture, Aug. 31, 1837.)

Read: Emerson's AMERICAN SCHOLAR..................Vol. 5, pp. 5-15

Ambroise Paré, a French army surgeon, devised in 1537 a method of treating battle wounds that superseded cautery. (See Reading Assignment for August 19th.)

AS GOOD, ALMOST, KILL A MAN AS KILL A GOOD BOOK.
—JOHN MILTON.

SEPTEMBER

Season of mists and mellow fruitfulness,
Close bosom-friend of the maturing sun;
Conspiring with him how to load and bless
With fruit the vines that round the thatch-eaves run. . .

KEATS (Vol. 41, p. 879)

1 Expelled from College, Founded a City

While at Oxford, Penn rejected the student's gown and thereby
created a furore. Later he founded a city where he sought to
put his new ideas into practice.

(Penn arrested for preaching in London, Sept. 1, 1670.)
Read from Penn's SOME FRUITS OF SOLITUDE..........Vol. 1, pp. 321-331

2 Too Great a Price for Love

While his soldiers fought the battle of Actium, Antony fled to
the arms of Cleopatra. By his flight he forfeited his right to an
empire. Dryden's story of Antony's love makes us realize the
folly of his infatuation for the Nile siren.

(Battle of Actium, Sept. 2, 31 B. C.)
Read from Dryden's ALL FOR LOVE.................Vol. 18, pp. 88-100

3 Seven Years to Reach England

Until 1783 the British refused to believe that the Liberty Bell
had rung. Then they signed a treaty formally recognizing the
Colonies as free and independent states.

(Treaty between England and the United States signed Sept. 3, 1783.)
Read: TREATY WITH GREAT BRITAIN (1783)..........Vol. 43, pp. 174-179

4 Voltaire Criticizes

Voltaire's daring courage led him to publish a series of letters
which contained unfavorable comparisons of French customs
with the English. For this he was threatened with the Bastille.

Read: Voltaire's LETTERS ON THE ENGLISH..............Vol. 34, pp. 85-93

5 Survival of the Fittest

Just as the individual has a definite length of life, so have species
a limited duration. The progress and transition of the world,
Darwin declares, will see the extinction of certain variants of
human life.

(Darwin first outlines his theory of natural selection, Sept. 5, 1857.)
Read from Darwin's ORIGIN OF SPECIES..............Vol. 11, pp. 353-357

September *Reading Guide*

6 The Pride of All Scotchmen

Many sons of Scotland have striven eagerly for the great place held by Sir Walter Scott. Carlyle describes the qualities that combined to make him the idol of his people and the master of historical romance.

Read Carlyle's SIR WALTER SCOTT..................Vol. 25, pp. 393-403

7 The King's Love

There she was undoing her hair—the loveliest woman the eyes of men ever beheld, the light of wooing in her regal eyes. A longing for her overwhelmed the warrior-king.

Read from DESTRUCTION OF DA DERGA'S HOSTEL......Vol. 49, pp. 199-209

8 When Europe Lay Under Ice

There was a time when the snow fell and did not melt in summer. Then from the frozen north there descended huge masses of ice that covered northern Europe and most of North America. Glaciers reveal a new world to us.

(Helmholtz died Sept. 8, 1894.)

Read from Helmholtz's ICE AND GLACIERS............Vol. 30, pp. 211-223

9 When Nature Beckons

"There are days during the year," says Emerson, "when the world of nature reaches perfection." Can anyone escape this call, especially in the glorious Indian Summer?

(Emerson retires from the ministry, Sept. 9, 1832.)

Read: Emerson's NATURE.........................Vol. 5, pp. 223-230

10 Famous Poet-Physician

One of America's famous New Englanders, Oliver Wendell Holmes, devoted his life principally to medicine. His name, however, was made famous through his poem, "Old Ironsides," by which he saved America's most famous battleship from destruction when her fighting days were ended.

Read: Holmes' POEMS.........................Vol. 42, pp. 1365-1370

11 Wages—Why and How Much?

What regulates wages, on what do they depend? Adam Smith, world's authority on economic problems, advances his theories on these matters.

Read from Adam Smith's WEALTH OF NATIONS.........Vol. 10, pp. 66-74

SEPTEMBER *Reading Guide*

12 Love Letters of Elizabeth Browning

In all literary history there is no happier love story than that of Elizabeth Barrett and Robert Browning. During their secret courtship Miss Barrett sent Browning many beautiful love letters written in verse.

(*Browning married Elizabeth Barrett, Sept. 12, 1846.*)
Read: SONNETS FROM THE PORTUGUESE............Vol. 41, pp. 923-932

13 Good That Came from a Game Pit

From cockfighting, bear baiting, and like sports, the wife of John Bunyan converted him to a life of humility and reverence. While imprisoned for preaching, he used his idle time in writing a fantastic story of a soul's salvation—probably the most famous allegory ever written.

(*John Bunyan liberated and pardoned, Sept. 13, 1672.*)
Read from Bunyan's PILGRIM'S PROGRESS..............Vol. 15, pp. 13-23

14 Dante and St. Peter

Dante, having journeyed through Hell and Purgatory, comes at last to St. Peter on his throne. St. Peter calls for the aid of St. James and St. John before passing final judgment on Dante's righteousness.

(*Dante died Sept. 14, 1321.*)
Read from Dante's DIVINE COMEDY................Vol. 20, pp. 387-395

15 Refused to Serve Three Terms

George Washington retired to private life in 1796, entrusting "the preservation of the Union" to the "love of liberty." His last appeal is a vital message to American citizens, as pertinent today as when he penned it.

(*George Washington published "Farewell Address," Sept. 15, 1796.*)
Read: Washington's FAREWELL ADDRESS.............Vol. 43, pp. 233-249

16 Penalty for Silence

"Such felons as stand mute [do not confess] are pressed to death by huge weights laid upon a board that lieth over their breast and a sharp stone under their backs." Old English punishments, recorded by Holinshed, make startling reading.

Read from HOLINSHED'S CHRONICLES................Vol. 35, pp. 363-370

SEPTEMBER *Reading Guide*

17 Romance on a New England Farm

"For of all sad words of tongue or pen, the saddest are these: 'It might have been.'" On this theme Whittier based the story of a fair farmer girl and a rich judge.

(Whittier died Sept. 17, 1892.)

Read: WHITTIER'S POEMS........................Vol. 42, pp. 1351-1364

18 Home After Storms and Adventures

"Every sight was full of beauty. We were coming back to our homes, and the signs of civilization from which we had been so long banished—" wrote Dana, as his ship entered Boston Harbor.

(Dana returns from two-year voyage, Sept. 18, 1836.)

Read from Dana's Two YEARS BEFORE THE MAST......Vol. 23, pp. 348-356

19 Humor That Survived Slavery

Held as a Moorish slave for five years, Cervantes was submitted to almost daily tortures. But even the horrors of slavery could not dull his sense of humor, as evinced by his most witty and amusing novel.

(Cervantes ransomed from slavery, Sept. 19, 1580.)

Read from Cervantes' DON QUIXOTE...................Vol. 14, pp. 48-54

20 Women's Rights in the Harem

The Koran defines the powers of a husband over his wives. Thus a woman unfaithful to her lord may be walled up alive.

(Mohammed arrives at Kuba after "The Flight," Sept. 20, 622.)

Read from THE KORAN.......................... Vol. 45, pp. 967-974

21 Æneas and the Old Witch

The Sybil, an old witch, personally conducts Æneas through the gate and into the jaws of hell, where terrors abound on every hand and frightful mysterious forms rule. There he is told of the greatness and glory that was to come.

(Virgil died Sept. 21, 19 B. C.)

Read from Virgil's ÆNEID.......................Vol. 13, pp. 207-218

22 A King for a Souvenir

In the days when kings rode to battle leading their troops it was possible to make good the boast of the doughboy: "I'll bring you a king for a souvenir."

(Froissart dates Battle of Poitiers, Sept. 22, 1356.)

Read from FROISSART'S CHRONICLES.................Vol. 35, pp. 42-53

September *Reading Guide*

23   Dying Concerns Every Man

The Romans made an art of dying. The Egyptians looked on death with complacency. Moderns fear it. Montaigne argues that the purpose of philosophy is to teach men how to die.

Read from Montaigne's To Learn How to Die.........Vol. 32, pp. 9-22

24   Citizens Lured from Their Homes

When the serpent of Minerva disappeared from her temple, the priests said that the goddess had left Athens for the sea. Moreover, the oracles urged the Athenians to seek safety in their ships. Themistocles prompted these deceits. Why?

Read from Plutarch's Themistocles.................Ol. 12, pp. 13-23

25   A Courtship of Twenty Years

John Stuart Mill in his autobiography boldly tells of his love for his friend's wife. After twenty years, she was freed from her first husband and was happily married to John Stuart Mill. Read the account of Mill's courtship.

Read from Mill's Autobiography..............Vol. 25, pp. 116-120, 149

26   And the World Rocked with Laughter

The gaunt lunatic, Don Quixote, saw the world through glasses colored with romanticism that had gone out of style hundreds of years before he was born. Cervantes made the world laugh at the exaggerated stories it had been devouring.

(Printing of Cervantes' "Don Quixote" licensed, Sept. 26, 1604.)
Read from Cervantes' Don Quixote.................Vol. 14, pp. 29-35

27   Pascal's Fundamentals of Religion

To-day we have Fundamentalists and Modernists, each striving for the same goal. Pascal, two hundred and fifty years ago, gave his precepts of the fundamentals of religious thought.

(Pascal confers with Descartes, Sept. 27, 1647.)
Read from Pascal's Thoughts....................Vol. 48, pp. 181-192

28   He Introduced the Germ

Proof that germs cause many contagious diseases was established by Louis Pasteur. His discoveries revolutionized modern science and lessened the ravages of every type of disease.

(Louis Pasteur died Sept. 28, 1895.)
Read: Pasteur's The Germ Theory.................Vol. 38, pp. 364-370

SEPTEMBER *Reading Guide*

29 **Prophet of 400 Million People**

Confucius was a Chinese magistrate in 500 B. C. He lost the favor of the Emperor and wandered from city to city, teaching and giving counsel. After his death, Emperor and people alike bowed before his shrine.

Read from SAYINGS OF CONFUCIUS.....................Vol. 44, pp. 5-14

30 **A Gentleman According to Emerson**

An etiquette book and a good tailor do not always produce a gentleman—neither does the Social Register include only gentlemen. Emerson by quaint stories tells how fashion and manners combine to make that rare product—a gentleman.

(*Emerson's first marriage, Sept. 30, 1829.*)

Read from Emerson's MANNERS.....................Vol. 5, pp. 199-208

Confucius was a Chinese magistrate and minister of crime in 500 B. C. Though an ancient lawyer, he had modern ideas of prison reform. (See Reading Assignment for September 29th.)

THE MASTER SAID: BY BREADTH OF READING AND THE TIES OF COURTESY A GENTLEMAN WILL ALSO KEEP FROM ERROR'S PATH.—CONFUCIUS.

OCTOBER

The skies they were ashen and sober;
The leaves they were crispèd and sere—
The leaves they were withering and sere. . .

POE (Vol. 42, p. 1230)

1 Princes To-day and Yesterday

To-day the chief duty of a prince is to be the nation's friend maker. Years ago princes desired supreme power and, by fair means or foul, strove for control. Machiavelli was a guide for such ambitious princes.

(Machiavelli's model prince sent to France as papal legate, Oct. 1, 1498.)
Read from Machiavelli's THE PRINCE.................Vol. 36, pp. 36-44

2 Veteran Tells of Indian War

Just before Darwin visited Bahia Blanca, an Indian insurrection had been ruthlessly put down. A veteran of the Indian war told Darwin how Indians had been treated.

(Darwin returns from South America, Oct. 2, 1836.)
Read from Darwin's VOYAGE OF THE BEAGLE........Vol. 29, pp. 107-111

3 Good Enough for Chaucer

When polite English society conversed in French—considering English a vulgar tongue, fit only for servants and working people—Chaucer, nevertheless, wrote poems in this "vulgar" English, which charm us because of their quaint words.

Read: CHAUCER'S POEMS...........................Vol. 40, pp. 11-20

4 His Mouth Full of Pebbles

The man who put pebbles in his mouth and orated to the sea, shaved one-half of his head so that he would be obliged to stay at home until he had perfected his oratory—a strange method of attaining eminence, but a successful one.

Read from Plutarch's DEMOSTHENES................Vol. 12, pp. 196-205

5 Amateur Athlete in Old Athens

A boxer in public games desired to study philosophy at Athens. There were no furnaces to tend, no tables to wait on, no books or magazines to peddle, yet this sturdy young Greek managed to work his way through college.

Read from Newman's UNIVERSITY LIFE AT ATHENS......Vol. 28, pp. 51-61

October *Reading Guide*

6 **The Atrocious Spectacle of October 6th**
Wakened by the death cries of her sentry, Marie Antoinette, Queen of France, fled by a secret passage from the fury of a vile mob. The royal family was arrested and taken to Paris to await their fate.
Read from Burke's REVOLUTION IN FRANCE..........Vol. 24, pp. 208-217

7 **An Uncanonized American Saint**
John Woolman was the foremost leader of the early Quakers and contributed much to the spiritual life of the American Colonies. He was a pioneer in the crusade against slavery.
(John Woolman died Oct. 7, 1772.)
Read from THE JOURNAL OF JOHN WOOLMAN..........Vol. 1, pp. 283-288

8 **Fielding's Parody Becomes History**
Fielding wrote a lengthy story to burlesque a novel of Richardson. But the travesty overshot its mark. Instead of a mere parody, it became a masterpiece.
(Henry Fielding died Oct. 8, 1764.)
Read: Fielding's PREFACE TO JOSEPH ANDREWS........Vol. 39, pp. 176-181

9 **Songs Shake the Walls of Jericho**
Do you know that many of your favorite hymns have echoed for hundreds of years through vast cathedrals, and resounded from the walls of Jericho during the Crusades?
(Newman, author of "Lead, Kindly Light," baptized Oct. 9, 1845.)
Read: LATIN HYMNS..............Vol. 45, pp. 546-556; also pp. 567-568

10 **A Fugitive in Boy's Clothes**
The romance-stricken Don Quixote sees a fair youth seated by the side of a stream, "his feet like two crystals, his hands like snowflakes." The youth was a charming girl!
(Cervantes aided in the capture of Tunis, Oct. 10, 1573.)
Read from Cervantes' DON QUIXOTE.................Vol. 14, pp. 252-266

11 **Æneas Flees from an Inconsolable Love**
Æneas, mythological founder of the Roman race, leaving Carthage and its lovely Queen Dido, was driven by a storm to the coast of Sicily. There the hospitality of King Acestes helped him to forget his relinquished love.
Read from Virgil's ÆNEID........................Vol. 13, pp. 178-188

OCTOBER *Reading Guide*

12 **Columbus' Letter Miraculously Found**
(*Columbus Day.*)
Historical documents, now priceless, were often used as wrapping paper. Rescued by chance was a letter of Columbus telling of his voyages—of the amazing bargains made with timid natives—of Amazon women who fought like men and made marriage treaties with cannibals.
Read: LETTER OF COLUMBUS........................Vol. 43, pp. 21-27

13 **Pagan Virtue Perpetuated**
A man of virtue, although a pagan, Marcus Aurelius ruled with benevolence and wisdom. Cruel in persecution of Christians as lawbreakers, no trace of this sternness appears in his writings.
Read from Marcus Aurelius' MEDITATIONS.............Vol. 2, pp. 193-199

14 **No Spice and Little Gold**
All colonies are founded to gain territory or treasure. Spain expected spice and gold from Columbus's expedition, but got no spice and little gold. Adam Smith tells the true motive of the colonizing Greeks, Romans, English, and Spaniards.
Read from Adam Smith's WEALTH OF NATIONS........Vol. 10, pp. 395-404

15 **First Families of America**
"They are a people smooth and clean of body because of continually washing themselves—they eat all their enemies whom they kill or capture." Amerigo Vespucci thus writes of the New World inhabitants.
(*Amerigo Vespucci returns from first American voyage, Oct. 15, 1498.*)
Read: VESPUCCI'S ACCOUNT OF HIS FIRST VOYAGE........Vol. 43, pp. 28-44

16 **When Medicine Was a Mystery**
Once physicians treated the sick with a mixture of medicine and charms. In those days medicine was regarded as a dark art like magic, and those practicing it formed guilds to protect themselves.
Read: HIPPOCRATES' OATH AND LAW....................Vol. 38, pp. 3-5

17 **Reason His Only Religion**
The religion of Thomas Browne—a liberal man in a most intolerant time—was not taken from either Rome or Geneva, but from his own reason.
(*Browne visited by Evelyn of "Evelyn Diary," Oct. 17, 1671.*)
Read from Browne's RELIGIO MEDICI................Vol. 3, pp. 253-265

OCTOBER *Reading Guide*

18 "If Winter Comes"

From the title of a recently popular novel, we know that one prominent fiction writer of to-day was inspired by the verses of Shelley. Many others have also felt the stirring vigor of his poetry. What is your reaction?

Read: SHELLEY'S POEMS.........................Vol. 41, pp. 829-835

19 Virtue in Smiles

Weep if you must. It is far better than to repress your tears. But Leigh Hunt finds greater virtue in cheerfulness. Fanciful and graceful—his writings exerted a wholesome influence on all nineteenth century journalism.

(James Henry Leigh Hunt born Oct. 19, 1784.)

Read: Hunt's ESSAYS.............................Vol. 27, pp. 285-295

20 Odysseus Adrift on a Raft

The gods met in council and decreed that Odysseus be set adrift. Poseidon, God of the Sea, shattered the raft and Odysseus was cast ashore to encounter further adventures.

Read from Homer's ODYSSEUS........................Vol. 22, pp. 68-80

21 No Fault to Find with Old Age

Cicero agrees with Browning that old age is the golden time of life, when the fruits of a well-spent life are harvested. Cicero, the wise Roman, welcomed old age for its gifts: wisdom, sound judgment, and contentment.

Read from Cicero's ON OLD AGE.....................Vol. 9, pp. 45-56

22 Swift's Love Problems

Swift was embarrassed by two women; Stella, whom he really loved, and Vanessa, with whom he had flirted and who had taken him seriously. Marriage to either one would break the heart of the other.

Read from Thackeray's JONATHAN SWIFT..............Vol. 28, pp. 23-28

23 When Cæsar Turned the Tables

When only a boy, Cæsar was captured by pirates. While awaiting ransom he entered into every sport and game with them. Once freed, he quickly returned with forces that captured the outlaws. Then he took deliberate revenge.

Read from Plutarch's CÆSAR.......................Vol. 12, pp. 264-273

OCTOBER *Reading Guide*

24 **Clytemnestra Meets Her Rival**

Cassandra knew through a prophetic vision that a sword would pierce her heart. Agamemnon, her captor, took her to his home where an avenging wife, Clytemnestra, awaited. The tragedies of the doom that requited the sins of the House of Atreus are among the most powerful ever written.

Read from Æschylus' AGAMEMNON....................Vol. 8, pp. 52-64

25 **It Greatly Encouraged Intrigue**

After the publication of Machiavelli's "The Prince," the Sultans became more addicted to strangling their brothers, tyrants became more merciless, and murderous plots increased. The influence of that book, as Macaulay points out, spread over Europe and Asia.

(*Thomas Babington Lord Macaulay born Oct. 25, 1800.*)

Read from Macaulay's MACHIAVELLI.................Vol. 27, pp. 363-372

26 **Franklin Learned the Secret**

Poor at twenty, rich at forty, internationally famous at fifty. Benjamin Franklin once walked the streets of Philadelphia alone, poor, and with no education. Yet he rose to be a leader because he learned the secret of careful reading.

(*Franklin made U. S. plenipotentiary in France, Aug. 26, 1778.*)

Read from Franklin's AUTOBIOGRAPHY.................Vol. 1, pp. 14-21

27 **Fruit of Seven Years' Silence**

Siddhartha Gautama, who became the god Buddha, renounced the world and spent seven years in meditation. Then one day, while sitting under a fig tree, he became inspired with exalted and sublime conceptions of life and death. The rest of his life was spent in teaching and converting mankind.

Read from BUDDHIST WRITINGS....................Vol. 45, pp. 661-674

28 **How Dice Taught Spelling**

Locke taught children by means of games. He tells of a game whereby children were taught to spell with dice on which the letters of the alphabet were pasted. This was more than 200 years before modern kindergarten methods. Today's children would respond to such wise direction as Locke recommends.

(*John Locke died Oct. 28, 1704.*)

Read: SOME THOUGHTS CONCERNING EDUCATION......Vol. 37, pp. 128-136

OCTOBER *Reading Guide*

29 **Genius Rises from a Stable**

(John Keats born Oct. 29, 1795.)

Though the son of a stable man, John Keats wrote the most exquisite and sublime poetry in our language. He was the friend of Shelley, Lord Byron, and the other literary leaders of the time— his genius recognized by all.

Read: KEATS' POEMS............................Vol. 41, pp. 874-882

30 **Geology's Greatest Benefactor**

Lyell has been called the founder of modern geology. Darwin, the master scientist, called him "Geology's Greatest Benefactor." Lyell's research revolutionized ideas on that subject.

Read from Lyell's THE PROGRESS OF GEOLOGY........Vol. 38, pp. 385-391

31 **Witches Walk To-night**

(All Hallows' Eve.)

Beware of magic! Once a year uneasy spirits are released and walk the earth from midnight until dawn. Spooks and goblins invade the most secure homes and the canniest must watch out for danger lurking in every dark corner.

Read from BURNS' POEMS.........................Vol. 6, pp. 110-119

John Locke taught spelling by means of dice with letters of the alphabet pasted on them. (See Reading Assignment for October 28th.)

THE FIRST TIME I READ AN EXCELLENT BOOK, IT IS TO ME JUST AS IF I HAD GAINED A NEW FRIEND.—GOLDSMITH.

NOVEMBER

When biting Boreas, fell and dour,
Sharp shivers thro' the leafless bow'r;
When Phœbus gies a short-liv'd glow'r,
Far south the lift,
Dim-dark'ning thro' the flaky show'r,
Or whirling drift.

BURNS (Vol. 6, p. 248)

1 Last Strokes of Shakespeare's Pen

Monsters of the earth, weird creatures of the air, magic romance, and shipwreck are mingled by a master hand in his thrilling drama. The fanciful, enchanting "Tempest" is the last work of the great bard of Stratford.

("*The Tempest*" performed at Queen Elizabeth's court, *Nov. 1, 1611.*)
Read from Shakespeare's THE TEMPEST..............Vol. 46, pp. 397-410

2 Journey Through a Hot Country

Dante recorded the awful scenes of a journey through the pits of the underworld, and wrote in such a vivid, realistic way that men tremble at the terrors depicted.

Read from Dante's DIVINE COMEDY...................Vol. 20, pp. 13-20

3 Letters to an Emperor

Pliny sought the advice of the Emperor Trajan for dealing with the Christians who were alarmingly on the increase. He casually relates how he had tortured two Christians.

Read from Pliny's LETTERS........................Vol. 9, pp. 404-406

4 Gold or Glory?

Polyeucte, an Armenian noble, wanted to become a Christian. If he were baptized, he would have to give up his high position, his wealth and his pagan wife. Was the heavenly crown worth this sacrifice?

Read from Corneille's POLYEUCTE...................Vol. 26, pp. 87-97

5 Costly Opinion on Divorce

A divorce always means trouble for some one. So with Sir Thomas More when he refused to agree with King Henry over the king's separation. More was made to pay one of the highest prices ever paid for a difference of opinion.

Read from Roper's LIFE OF SIR THOMAS MORE.........Vol. 36, pp. 89-99

November *Reading Guide*

6 A Genius Needs Few Tools

Two sticks, a table, and a pail were the commonplace implements used by Michael Faraday to demonstrate great scientific truths.

(Faraday sends "Experimental Researches" to Royal Society, Nov. 6, 1845.)
Read: Faraday's FORCE OF GRAVITATION...............Vol. 30, pp. 13-21

7 The Voice from a Stone-Dead City

Suddenly all the sinful city's inhabitants were turned to stone. When a beautiful woman from Bagdad came to the dead city, night overtook her there. Sleeping in the palace, she was awakened by a man's voice calling.

Read from THE THOUSAND AND ONE NIGHTS.........Vol. 16, pp. 100-107

8 Blind But Unconquered

Milton's indomitable courage kept him at his work even after he lost his sight. Blind, he dictated a sequel to his "Paradise Lost," which he called "Paradise Regained."

(John Milton died Nov. 8, 1674.)
Read from Milton's PARADISE REGAINED...............Vol. 4, pp. 359-369

9 Once War Songs, Now Pious Prayers

The Psalms have been an inspiration to men in many ages. They have become so associated with the peaceful spirit of Christianity that we forget some of them were once war songs and songs of triumph.

Read from THE PSALMS.........................Vol. 44, pp. 318-327

10 A Poet Who Piped for His Supper

Goldsmith traveled through Belgium, France, and Italy, winning his daily bread by playing at farmhouses. He wrote the most brilliant comedy, the best novel, and the finest poem of his age.

(Oliver Goldsmith born Nov. 10, 1728.)
Read: Goldsmith's THE DESERTED VILLAGE.........Vol. 41, pp. 509-520

11 America's Doughboy Glorified
(Armistice Day)

The youth of America—typified in the doughboy of the past war—was gloriously portrayed by Walt Whitman. He also sang of the vast plains and the beauty of America.

Read: WHITMAN'S POEMS.......................Vol. 42, pp. 1402-1412

NOVEMBER *Reading Guide*

12 **Story of the First Dresses**

Milton's version tells how the Serpent induced Eve to eat the forbidden fruit. Eve offered it to Adam. Then they became conscious for the first time that they were not clothed.

(John Milton married second wife, Nov. 12, 1656.)

Read from Milton's PARADISE LOST.................Vol. 4, pp. 278-290

13 **When Carthage Was Monte Carlo**

Carthage was the playground of the ancient world. In that city of many sins, Augustine was a leader of the revels. His conversion to Christianity amazed those who knew him.

(St. Augustine born Nov. 13, 354.)

Read from the CONFESSIONS OF ST. AUGUSTINE.........Vol. 7, pp. 31-38

14 **He Worried About It**

We wonder if the man who worried about the "scientifical" prediction that "The sun's heat will give out in ten million years more," had read Lyell on the gradual changes in the earth's surface.

(Sir Charles Lyell born Nov. 14, 1797.)

Read: Lyell's UNIFORMITY OF CHANGE..............Vol. 38, pp. 398-405

15 **Food Profiteers 300 Years Ago**

Food profiteering was as active in plague-stricken Milan 300 years ago as in modern times. Shops were stormed for food. Read how the Council strove heroically to fix fair rates.

(Sale of corn and flour regulated in Milan, Nov. 15, 1629.)

Read from Manzoni's I PROMESSI SPOSI.............Vol. 21, pp. 450-460

16 **Just Before the Gold Rush**

When the glorious Western coast was only partly settled, Dana visited the Presidios. He saw frontier life at a time when Spanish splendor still gilded California.

Read from TWO YEARS BEFORE THE MAST...........Vol. 23, pp. 164-168

17 **At Thirty Scott Began to Write**

Are you curious about famous people, their lives, habits, personalities? Carlyle discusses the intimate life of his illustrious countryman, and reveals Scott, the man, and Scott, the genius who entertained Christendom with his stories.

(Scott writes dedication of "Ivanhoe," Nov. 17, 1817.)

Read: Carlyle's SIR WALTER SCOTT.................Vol. 25, pp. 410-420

NOVEMBER *Reading Guide*

18 Apple or Son the Arrow's Mark
The arrow shot from his bow with a twang and whizzed through the air. Tell covered his eyes, fearing to see where the arrow hit. Then the shout of triumph, a shout of the people and not of the tyrant—but the end was not yet.
(*William Tell incident, legendary date, Nov. 18, 1307.*)
Read from Schiller's WILHELM TELL.............Vol. 26, pp. 441-449

19 No Man Knows His Resting Place
A barge with black sails bearing three black robed queens with crowns of gold carried away the dying King Arthur. Will they bring him back and fulfill Merlin's prophecy?
(*Queen Victoria appointed Tennyson poet laureate, Nov. 19, 1850.*)
Read: Tennyson's MORTE D'ARTHUR.............Vol. 42, pp. 986-992

20 Old Stories Ever New
When the cold winds howled about the thatched huts of the German peasant, the mother drew her children to her side and told them stories. Collected and retold by the Grimm brothers, these stories have perennial charm.
Read from GRIMM'S FAIRY TALES.............Vol. 17, pp. 90-98

21 Bargains in Wives
The beautiful daughters of the Circassians were in demand for the seraglios of the Turkish Sultan. Voltaire tells how these beauties were protected from smallpox centuries before modern vaccination.
(*Voltaire ill with smallpox, Nov., 1723.*)
Read from Voltaire's LETTERS.............Vol. 34, pp. 93-97

22 How a Queen Died for Love
Deserted by her lover, Queen Dido applied to her heart the only balm that could ease her pain.
Read from Virgil's ÆNEID.............Vol. 13, pp. 167-177

23 Less Than Star Dust
According to Pascal, a man is not even as significant as a speck of star dust in the universe. Pascal's thoughts on the subject are startling to the modern reader, and they furnish rich food for the imagination.
(*Pascal begins writing his "Thoughts," Nov. 23, 1654.*)
Read from PASCAL'S THOUGHTS.............Vol. 48, pp. 26-36

NOVEMBER *Reading Guide*

24 The Book that Upset Tennessee

The signal for the beginning of a great controversy, still raging, was the publication of Darwin's "Origin of Species." This was the first complete statement of the evolution theory, which had been privately advanced but never publicly taught. A new epoch in science dates from this great work.

(*"Origin of Species" published Nov. 24, 1859.*)
Read from Darwin's ORIGIN OF SPECIES . . . . Vol. 11, pp. 23-30

25 Cupid as a Shoemaker

We are indebted to Thomas Dekker for one of the most humorous characters in all Elizabethan literature; namely, Simon Eyre, an old shoemaker whose affairs became hilariously involved with those of the gentry.

Read from Dekker's THE SHOEMAKER'S HOLIDAY . . . . . . Vol. 47, pp. 469-483

26 Shakespeare Should Be Heard

Charles Lamb, favorite essayist, thought that no stage could do justice to Shakespeare's tragedies. He advocated reading the plays, and with the imagination costuming the players and building the gorgeous scenery in a way equaled by no scene painter or costumer.

Read: Lamb ON THE TRAGEDIES OF SHAKSPERE . . . . . . Vol. 27, pp. 299-310

27 What Land is This?

In wondrous Utopia pearls and precious stones were used as playthings for little children. Gold rings and bracelets were only worn by outcasts, while great golden chains shackled criminals and felons. When ambassadors from foreign lands came in fine raiment, the Utopians treated the plainest dressed as the greatest; the others seemed to them like children.

Read from Sir Thomas More's UTOPIA . . . . Vol. 36, pp. 191-204

28 Poems Made from Visions

"To see a world in a grain of sand, and a heaven in a wild flower—"
Such was the exaltation of the mysticism of William Blake, who reflected in his poetry the ecstasy of his visions. Simplicity is the keynote of his genius.

(*William Blake born Nov. 28, 1757.*)
Read: BLAKE'S POEMS . . . . Vol. 41, pp. 583-592

November *Reading Guide*

29 How Ideas Originate

Did you ever stop to think just how you thought? What inner emotions, what outer influences make up the fathomless depths of mind and intellect? Hume explains how we draw our thoughts, then clumsily put them into tangible shape called ideas.

Read: Hume's OF THE ORIGIN OF IDEAS.............Vol. 37, pp. 299-303

30 "Don'ts" for Conversation

To harp on one's illnesses, giving all the symptoms and circumstances, has been a blemish on conversation for ages. Two hundred years ago Swift complained of persons who continually talked about themselves.

(Jonathan Swift born Nov. 30, 1667.)

Read: Swift's ESSAY ON CONVERSATION.................Vol. 27, pp. 91-98

Michael Faraday taught scientific truths by everyday methods. By the use of two sticks, a table and a pail he demonstrated that the "center of gravity must remain within the base." (See Reading Assignment for November 6th.)

NO MAN SHOULD THINK SO HIGHLY OF HIMSELF AS TO THINK HE CAN RECEIVE BUT LITTLE LIGHT FROM BOOKS.

—JOHNSON.

DECEMBER

When icicles hang by the wall
And Dick the shepherd blows his nail,
And Tom bears logs into the hall,
And milk comes frozen home in pail. . .

SHAKESPEARE (Vol. 40, p. 262)

1 Are Skeptics Faulty Thinkers?
Offhand we say a skeptic is one who doubts everything. But does he? And are his doubts caused by too much learning, or too little? Berkeley presents both sides of skepticism.
Read from Berkeley's THREE DIALOGUES............Vol. 37, pp. 189-199

2 Practical Jokes in King Arthur's Day
Attacked in fun by two masked knights, Sir Galahad smote one so that both horse and rider went down. Turning on the other jester, he slashed open his helmet.
Read from THE HOLY GRAIL.......................Vol. 35, pp. 128-134

3 Met the Gods of Ten Thousand Worlds
After three awesome messengers have issued three warnings, the gods of ten thousand worlds decide who is to be the new Buddha. Then the parents, the conception, the birth of the god-child demand constant vigilance.
Read: THE BIRTH OF THE BUDDHA.................Vol. 45, pp. 603-612

4 The Queen Weds a Poor Stranger
Æneas and Dido, world-famous lovers, while hunting in the forest, were trapped in a cave by a furious storm. There the marriage between the proud African queen and the homeless wanderer was completed.
Read from Virgil's ÆNEID........................Vol. 13, pp. 152-162

5 Poems by an Artist's Model
So beautiful that many painters sought her for a model— Christina Rossetti, sister of the famous poet, Dante Rossetti, combined with her unusual beauty a rare poetic sense.
(Christina Georgina Rossetti born Dec. 5, 1830.)
Read: CHRISTINA ROSSETTI'S POEMS...............Vol. 42, pp. 1181-1183

DECEMBER *Reading Guide*

6 **Moralizing as a Seductive Art**
"The Vision of Mirza" and "Westminster Abbey," first printed in "The Spectator," are examples of Addison's wondrous gift of expression. He leads us to higher realms.
(Last issue of "The Spectator" published Dec. 6, 1712.)
Read: Addison's Essays...............................Vol. 27, pp. 73-80

7 **What Cicero Least Expected**
After being governor of Sicily, Cicero returned to Rome expecting a hero's welcome. When he asked what the Romans thought of his recent achievements, he received an astounding answer.
(Cicero slain by Mark Antony's soldiers, Dec. 7, 43 B. C.)
Read from Plutarch's CICERO........................Vol. 12, pp. 222-231

8 **Dream Women Shaped His Destiny**
De Quincy imagined that three women were sent to him so that he might know the depths of his soul. Real women could not have wielded greater influence. It is fortunate that everyone does not meet these weird women.
(Thomas De Quincy died Dec. 8, 1859.)
Read: LEVANA AND OUR LADIES OF SORROW...........Vol. 27, pp. 319-325

9 **Slavery's Last Stand**
By the Fugitive Slave Act of 1850 stringent laws were made to prevent assistance being given to any slaves attempting to escape. The antislavery answer to these laws was a perfection of the "Underground Railroad."
Read: THE FUGITIVE SLAVE ACT.....................Vol. 43, pp. 306-312

10 **Benvenuto Boasts of Gallantry**
Taking offense at a soldier who made advances toward his favorite lady, Cellini jumped from the window, knife in hand, to avenge himself. This incident was recorded with characteristic conceit by Cellini in his amazing diary.
Read from CELLINI's AUTOBIOGRAPHY..................Vol. 31, pp. 62-72

11 **The Most Dashing Figure in Athens**
The handsome Alcibiades, cunning in politics, bold in war, was the lion of Athenian society until he violated the secrets of a mysterious religious cult. Then all outraged Athens united to dash their idol to the ground.
Read from Plutarch's ALCIBIADES...................Vol. 12, pp. 106-117

DECEMBER *Reading Guide*

12 How the Glorious News was Carried to Aix

Three brave men began the heroic ride from Ghent to Aix. Only one man arrived to tell the thrilling story of the tempestuous ride. In one of his most bewitching poems, in lines that haunt the memory, Browning retells the story.

(*Robert Browning died Dec. 12, 1889.*)

Read: BROWNING'S POEMS......................Vol. 42, pp. 1066-1068

13 To the South Seas with the Gallant Drake

A famous voyage was Sir Francis Drake's around the world. Drake's crew, the first white men to visit many parts of the world, received amazing receptions from the natives.

(*Sir Francis Drake embarked for South Seas, Dec. 13, 1577.*)

Read from DRAKE'S VOYAGE ROUND THE WORLD......Vol. 33, pp. 199-208

14 Pastoral Poems and Politics

The many-sided Marvell, who wielded a pen that was both feared and courted, is seen at his best in stirring verse. "A Garden," "Prospect of Flowers," with the "Horatian Ode upon Cromwell," show the power of his genius.

(*Marvell entered Cambridge, Dec. 14, 1633.*)

Read: MARVELL'S POEMS........................Vol. 40, pp. 370-379

15 Odysseus Talks with Ghosts

This is another of those marvelous and unforgetable tales of the wandering Odysseus. The fantasy takes him into regions where he discourses with deceased heroes.

Read from Homer's ODYSSEY......................Vol. 22, pp. 145-153

16 How Man's Courtship Differs from Animal's

Beauty is an important factor in the attraction between man and woman. It is knowing beauty that differentiates man from the animals, which only require that their mates be of the same species.

Read from Burke's THE SUBLIME AND BEAUTIFUL......Vol. 24, pp. 37-48

17 Dies on the Eve of Her Son's Conversion

The mother of St. Augustine prayed unceasingly for her son's conversion. The most touching, most soul-revealing writing St. Augustine did is in the description of his mother's death.

Read from CONFESSIONS OF ST. AUGUSTINE............Vol. 7, pp. 150-160

December *Reading Guide*

18 **For a Gentleman**

Every schoolboy asks: "What's the use of learning Latin?" John Locke, one of the greatest educators of all time, maintains that Latin is absolutely essential to a well-bred gentleman, and explains why.

Read from Some Thoughts Concerning Education . . Vol. 37, pp. 136-145

19 **Samson Finds a Champion**

The mighty Samson was blinded while a captive of the Philistines. He sought revenge—a revenge devastating and costly. Milton, himself a giant of intellect, blind and imprisoned, wrote of this sightless giant of other days.

(Milton released from prison, Dec. 19, 1660.)
Read: Milton's Samson Agonistes . . . . Vol. 4, pp. 444-459

20 **Egypt Visited by the First Reporter**

All phases of life were pictured by Herodotus in his history. Like a modern newspaper reporter, he combines weird stories, scandals, and battle accounts with descriptions of places, persons, and sights about town.

Read from Herodotus' An Account of Egypt . . . . Vol. 33, pp. 7-17

21 **"Madam Bubble" Not to Be Discouraged**

"Madam Bubble," or this vain world, presented both herself and her purse to the wayfarer. Repulsed and scorned, yet she serenely flaunts her bribes enticingly before his bewildered eyes.

(John Bunyan made leader of Non-Conformist congregation, Dec. 21, 1671.)
Read from Bunyan's Pilgrim's Progress . . . . Vol. 15, pp. 306-318

22 **Rubbing Noses in New Zealand**

Darwin, in exploring New Zealand, finds cannibalism, tattooing, and many weird customs among the natives. Instead of shaking hands, the salutation is by rubbing noses.

(Darwin visits New Zealand natives, Dec. 22, 1835.)
Read from Darwin's Voyage of the Beagle . . . . Vol. 29, pp. 425-434

23 **Saved from a Bonfire of Books**

If all the books in the world were on fire, some men would risk their lives to save certain priceless writings: the world's classics. Sainte-Beuve here tells why.

(Sainte-Beuve born Dec. 23, 1804.)
Read: Sainte-Beuve's What Is a Classic? . . . . Vol. 32, pp. 121-133

December *Reading Guide*

24 Christmas Made a Dull Day

Before the Reformation in England almost every third day was a holy day. But the Puritans abolished all the holy days, even Christmas.

Read from HOLINSHED'S CHRONICLES............... Vol. 35, pp. 266-270

25 The Christmas Story
(Christmas Day.)

Luke was a Greek physician, a man of culture, trained in the best universities of the ancient world. He became imbued with the spirit of Christ, and wrote the most beautiful story of the birth and life of Jesus.

Read from the GOSPEL OF ST. LUKE................. Vol. 44, pp. 357-360

26 Silence Cost Her a Kingdom

Cordelia, daughter of old King Lear, could not convince her father of her love for him. Afterward, when misfortunes made him accept her aid, he learned too late of her real devotion.

("King Lear" presented at Queen Elizabeth's court, Dec. 26, 1606.)
Read from Shakespeare's KING LEAR............... Vol. 46, pp. 288-300

27 Million-Year-Old Islands

It was the new-old lands that Darwin visited on his voyage of the "Beagle." The strange specimens of prehistoric life he saw there made the world gape and shudder.

(Charles Darwin begins voyage in the "Beagle," Dec. 27, 1831.)
Read from Darwin's VOYAGE OF THE BEAGLE......... Vol. 29, pp. 376-389

28 Ho! for the Spanish Main!

Drake with a fleet of twenty-five ships and twenty-three hundred men sets sail to plunder and lay waste Spain's treasure hoards in the New World. Gold and silver bar, nuggets and jewels awaited the bold adventurers.

Read from DRAKE'S GREAT ARMADA................. Vol. 33, pp. 229-240

29 These Guests Outstayed Their Welcome

After twenty years' absence, Odysseus returned home to find his house filled with strangers rioting and wasting his treasure. Crafty Odysseus, with the aid of his son and the gods, devised a bold plan to rid his home of the unwelcome guests.

Read from Homer's ODYSSEY..................... Vol. 22, pp. 296-309

December *Reading Guide*

30 **Dana Meets a Tattooed Sailor**

Dana's description of the picturesque, pre-gold-rush California is unique. While he was on the Pacific coast he met a British sailor who was elaborately tattooed and of an unforgetable appearance and personality.

Read from Dana's Two Years Before the Mast........Vol. 23, pp. 77-86

31 **Curiosity and Interest as Guides to Reading**

The most unhappy man, Carlyle says, is the man who has no real work—no interest in life. To avoid this miserable state, he advises faithful and diligent reading along the lines dictated by curiosity and interest.

Read from Carlyle's Inaugural Address.............Vol. 25, pp. 364-374

Basic unity of religions is strikingly revealed in the similarity between the Ten Commandments of Moses and the Precepts of Buddha. (See Reading Assignment for December 3rd.)

THE FOUNTAIN OF WISDOM FLOWS THROUGH BOOKS.

—Greek Proverb.

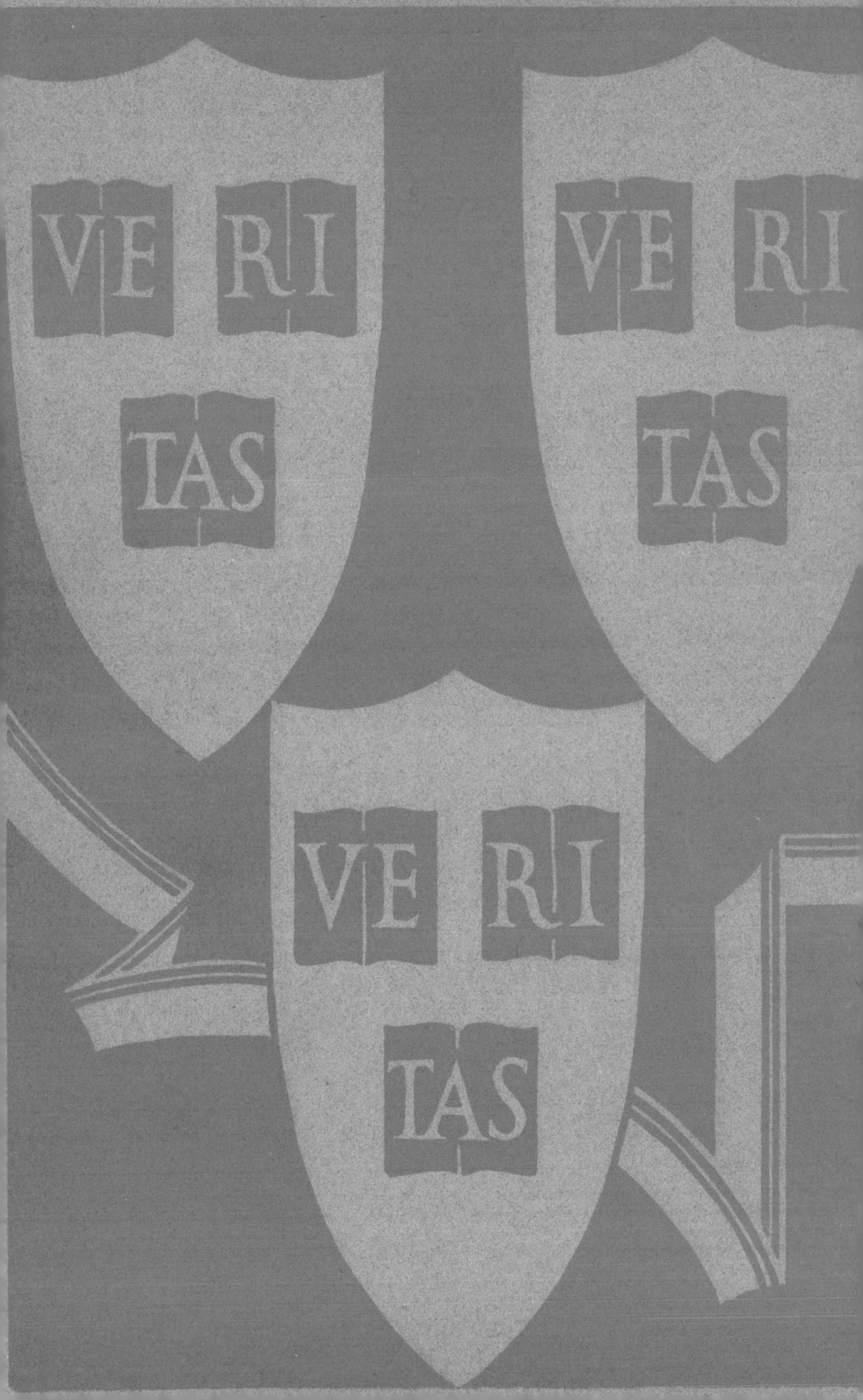
VE RI TAS
VE RI TAS
VE RI TAS